Cheeky Sweary Animals

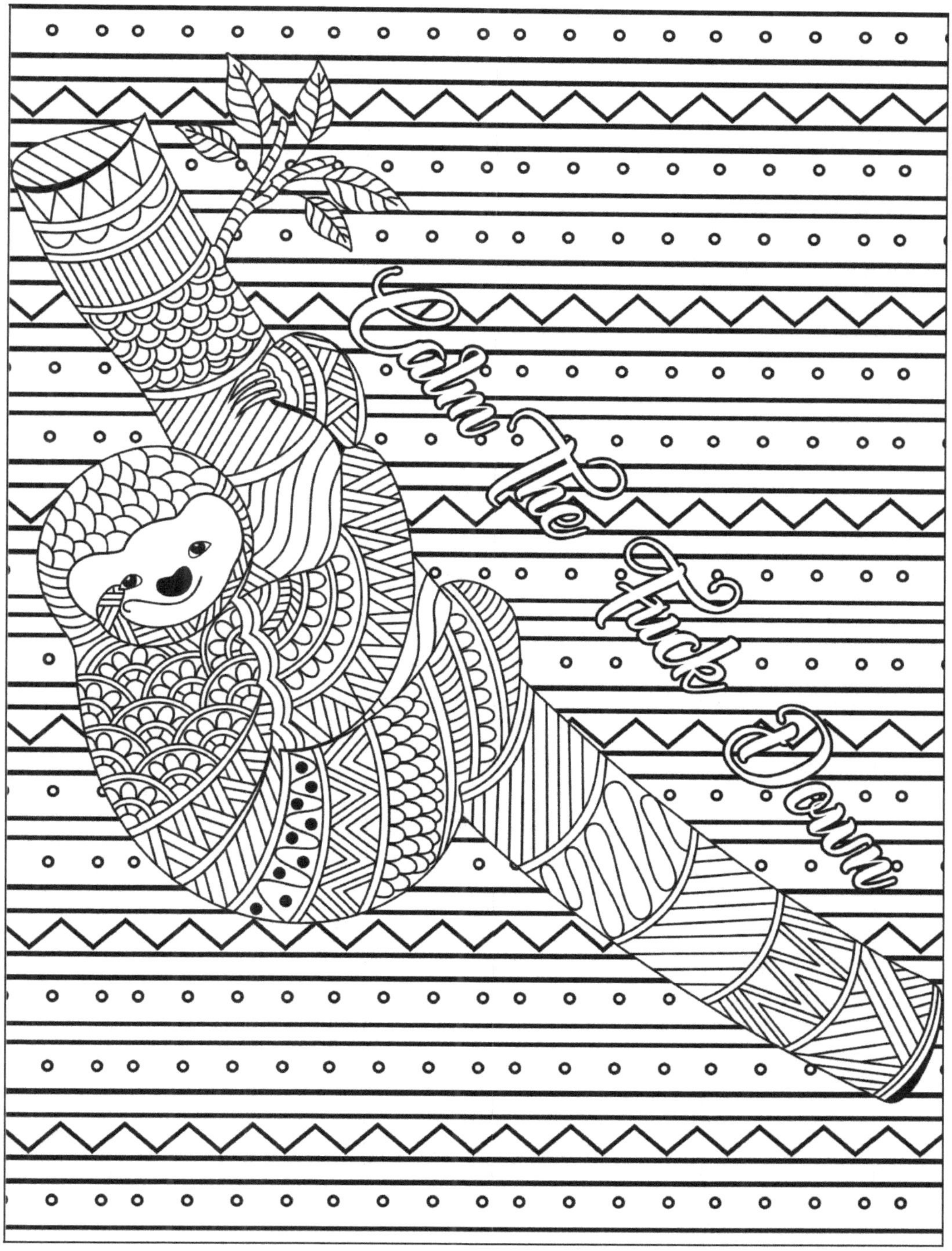

Swear Word Coloring Book For Adults

Copyright 2017 'Swear Words Coloring Books'
All Rights Reserved. This book or any part of it may not be used
in any matter whatsoever without the express written permission
of the publisher except for the use of brief quotations in a book review

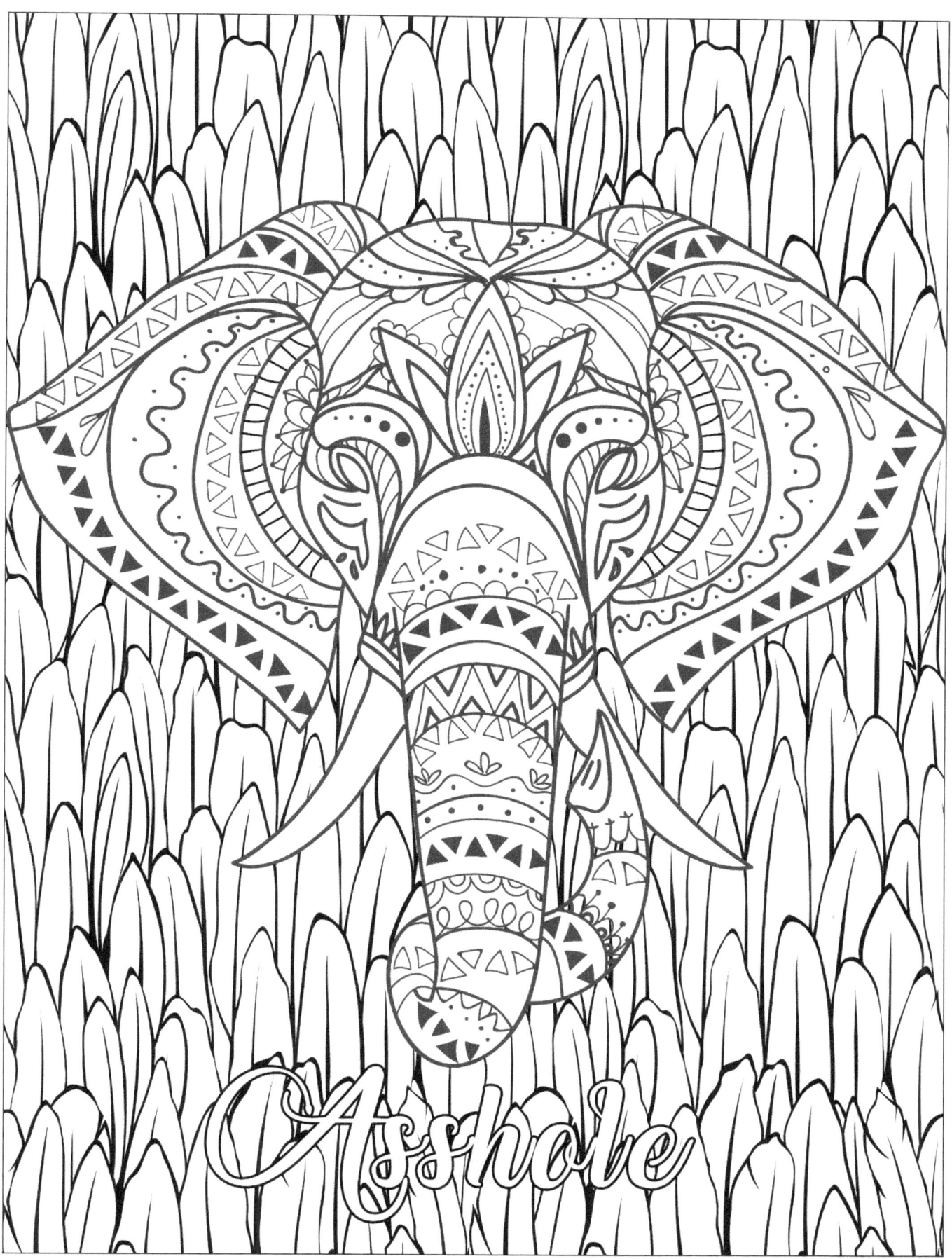

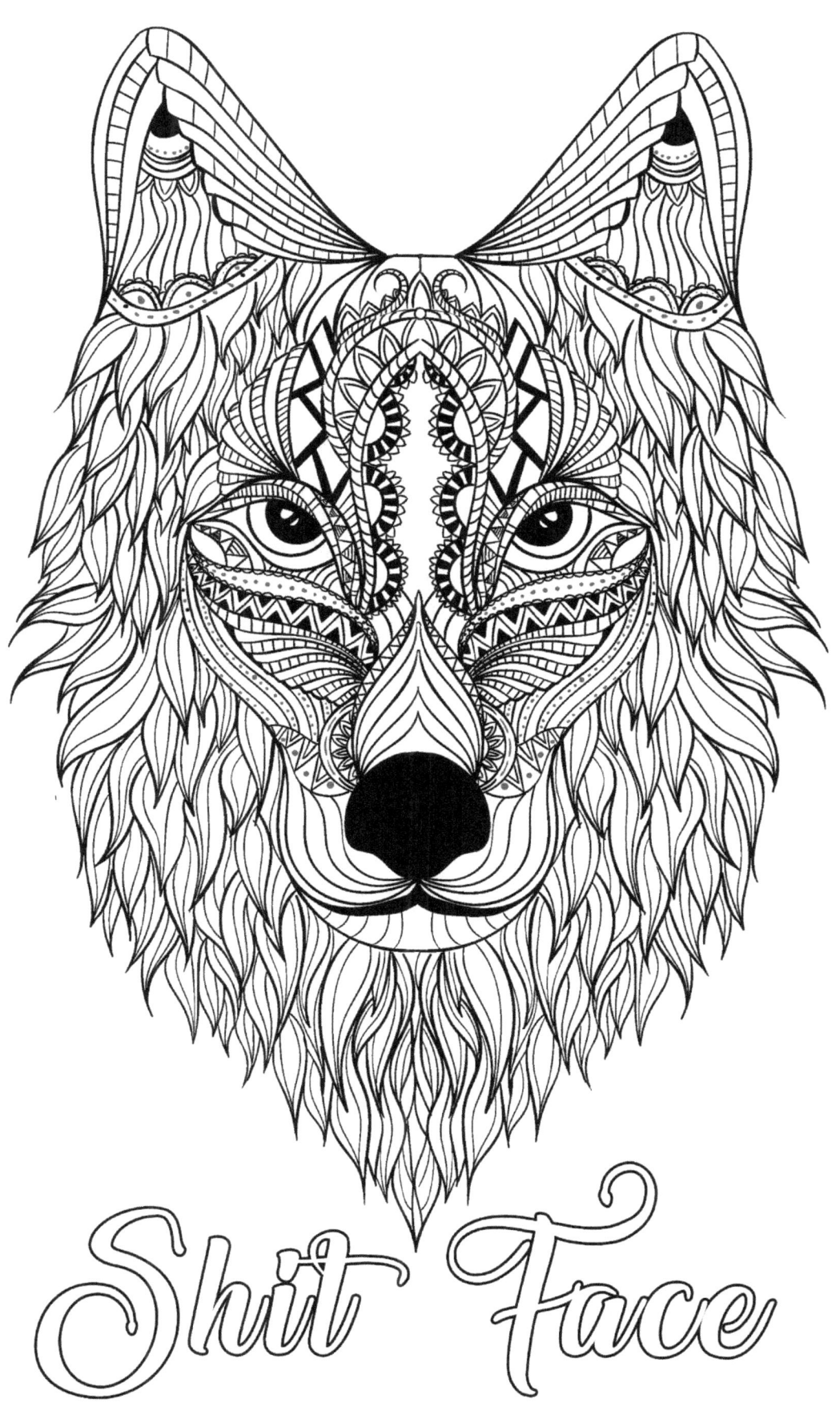

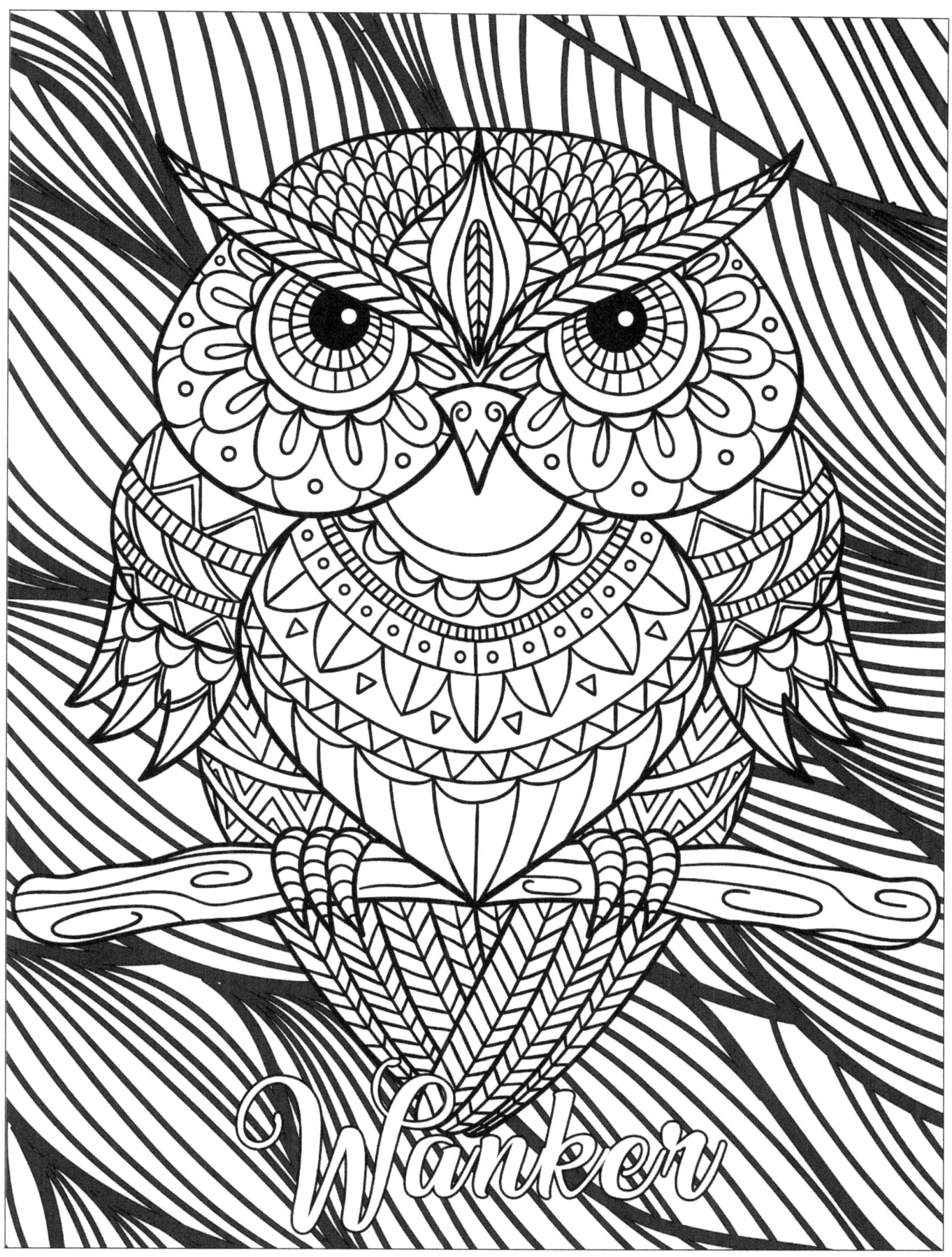

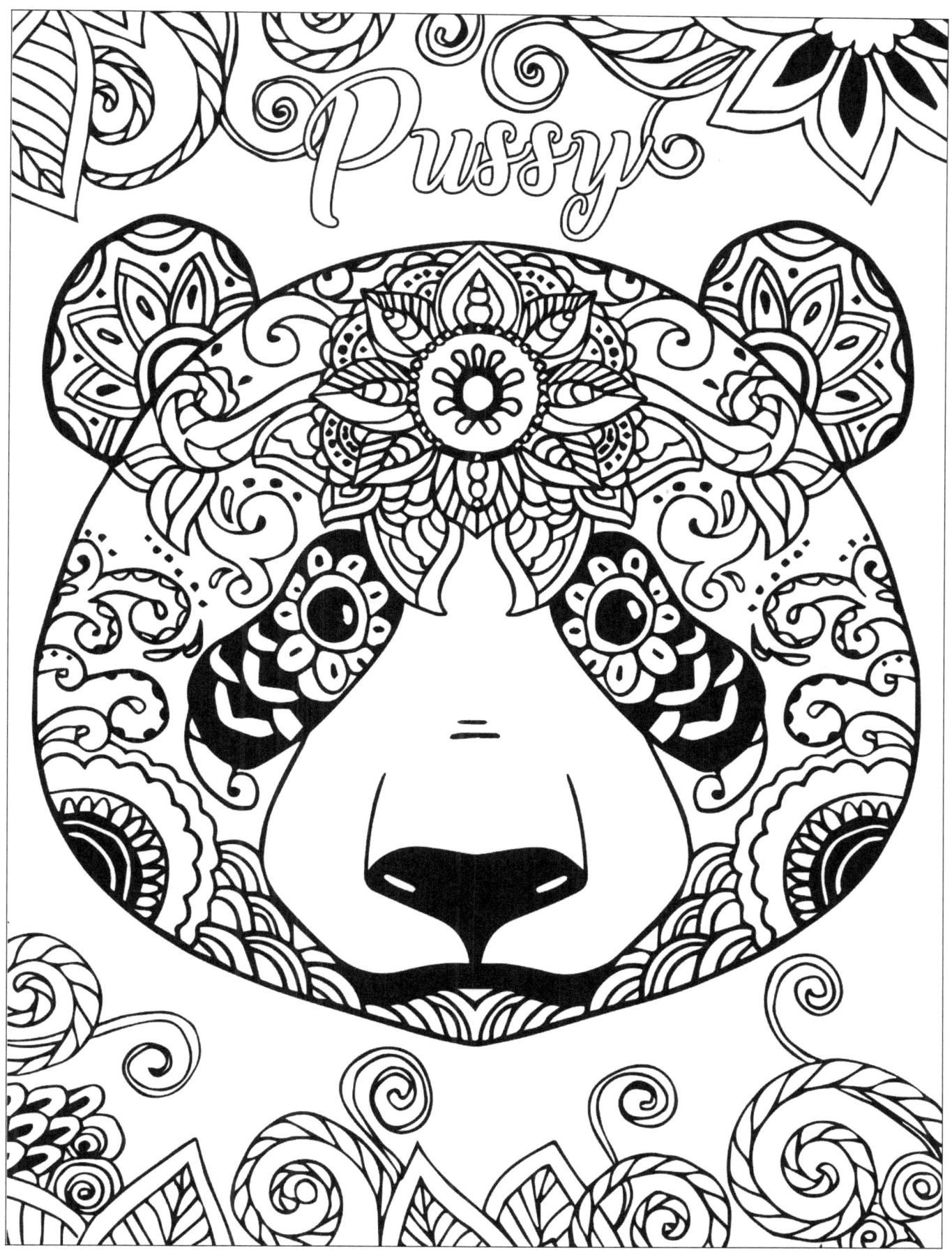

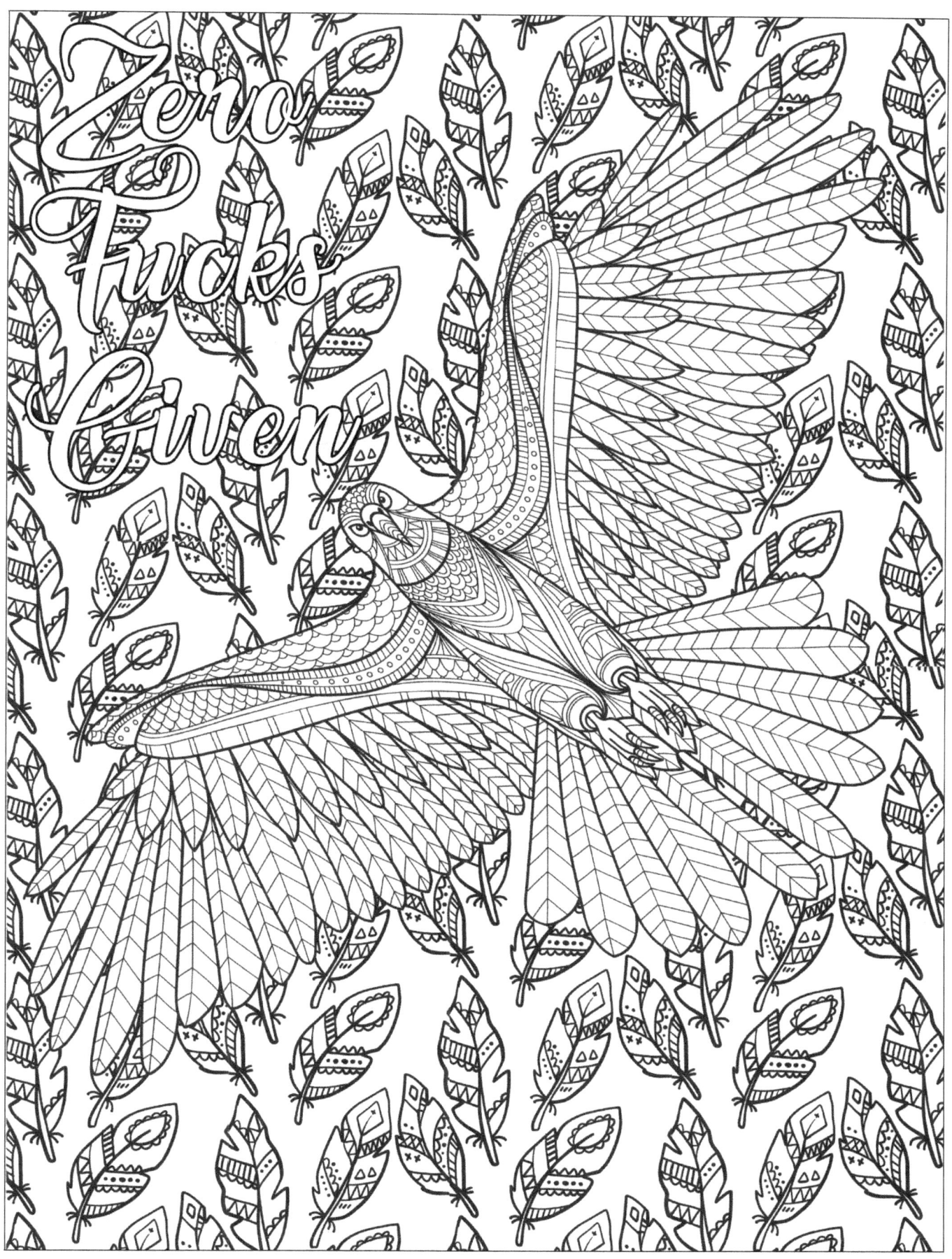

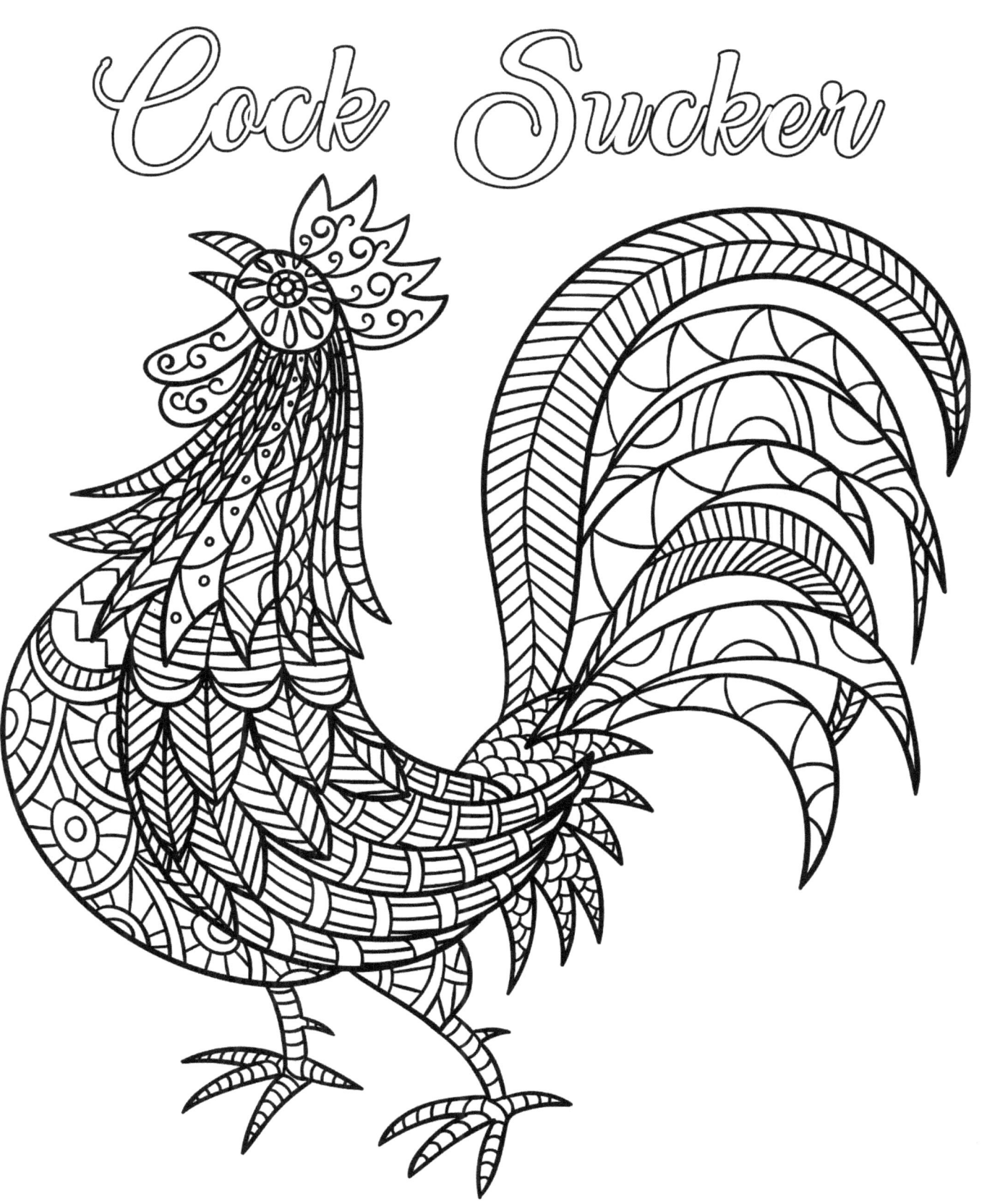

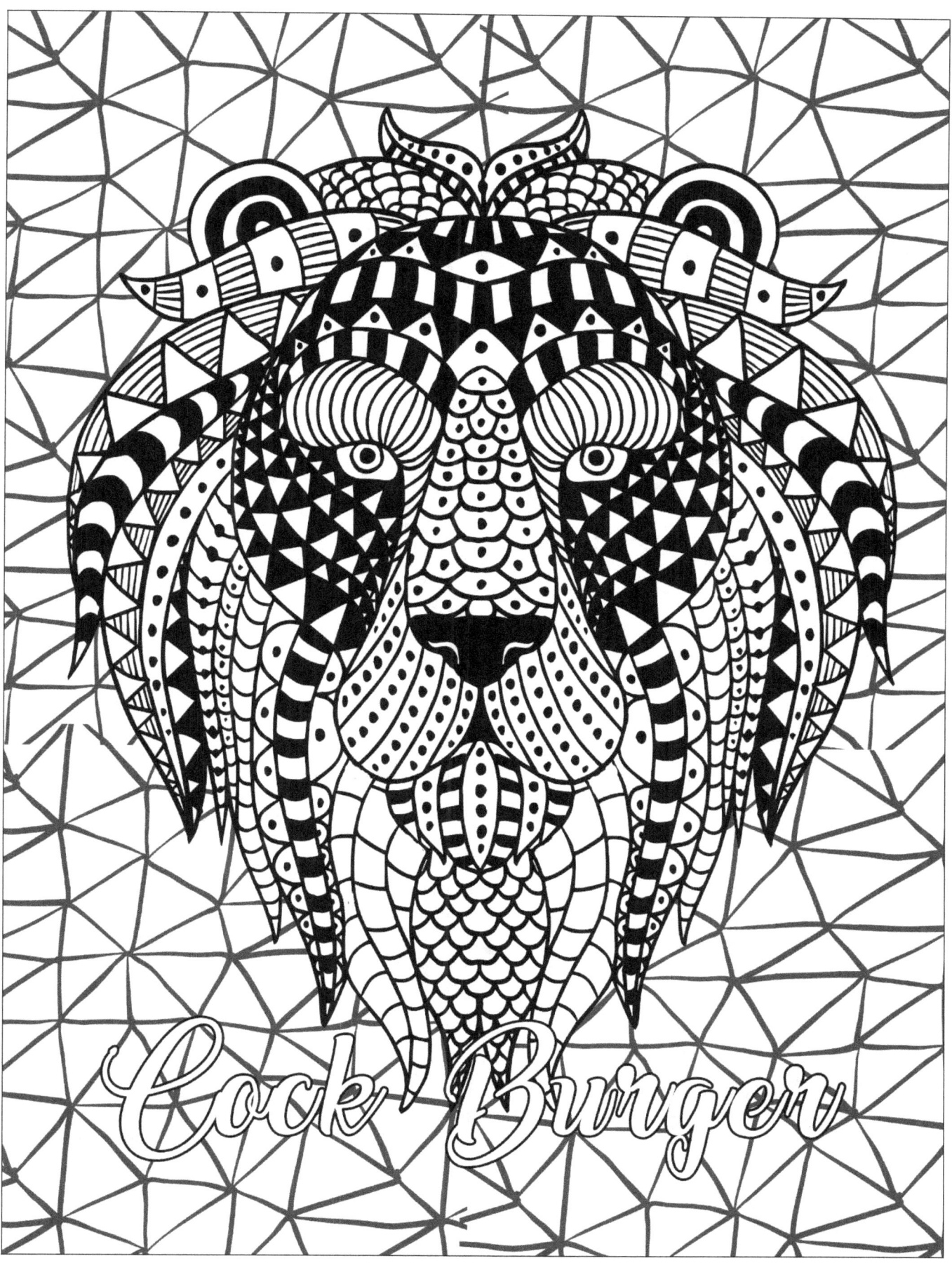

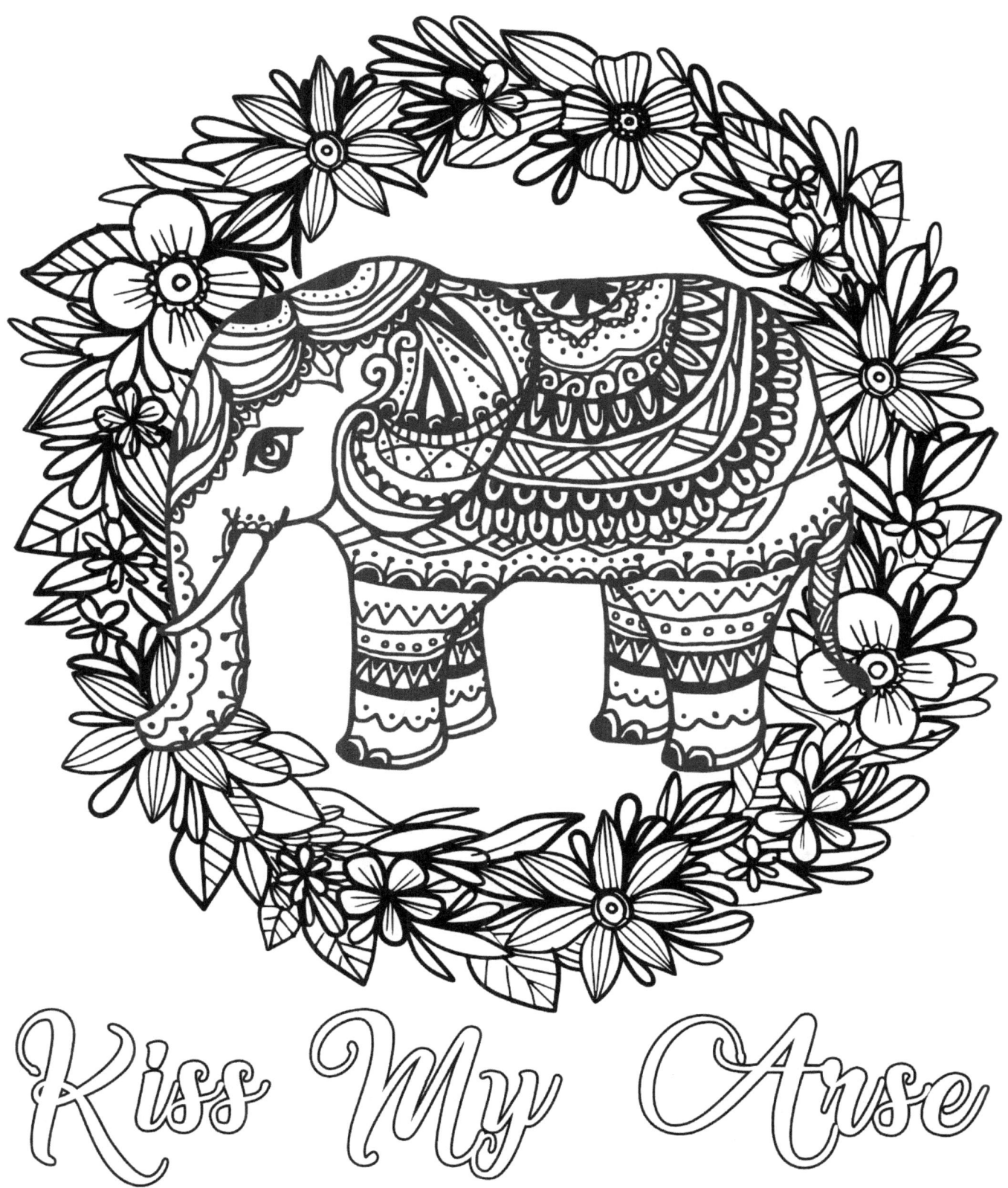

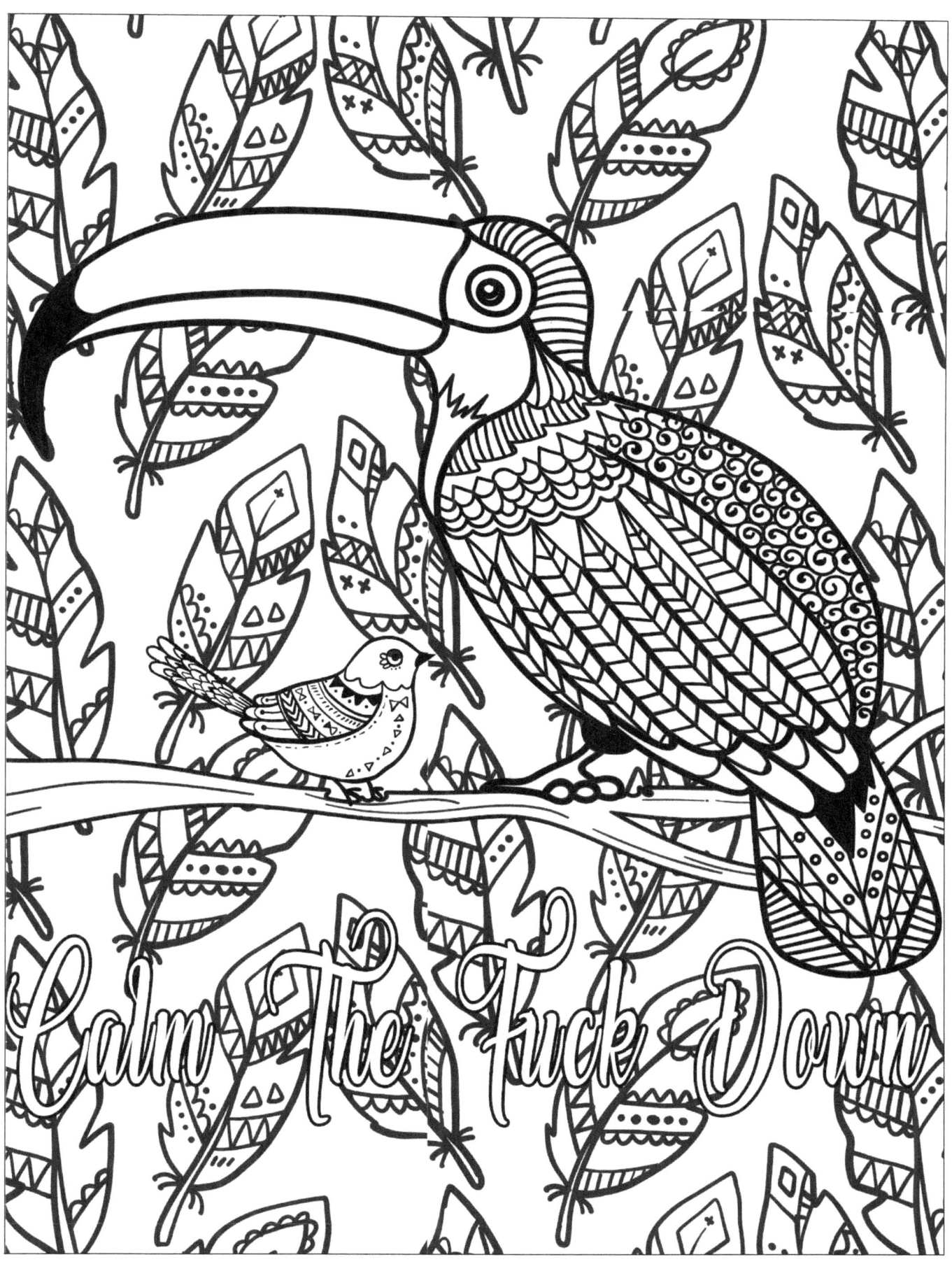

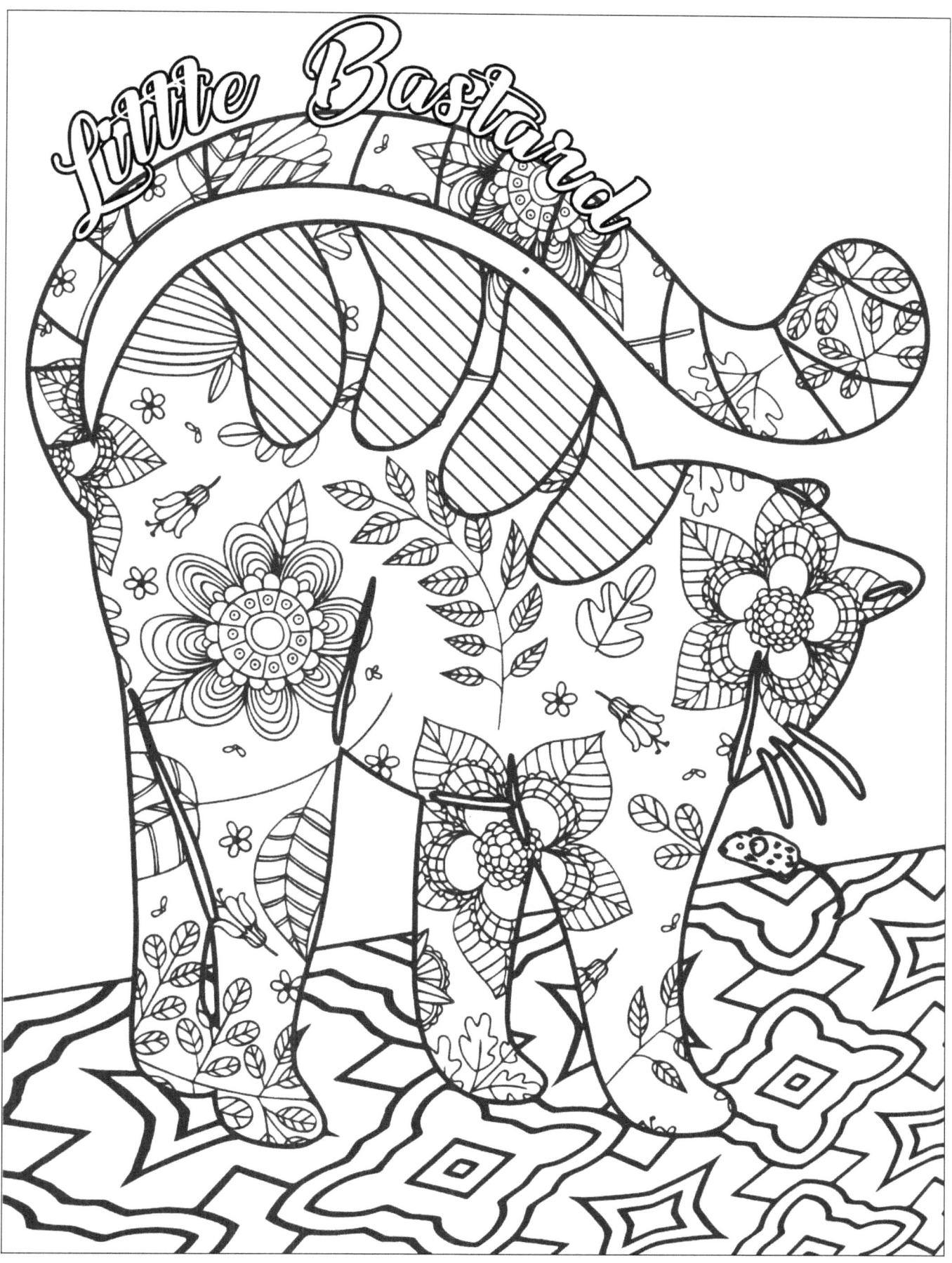

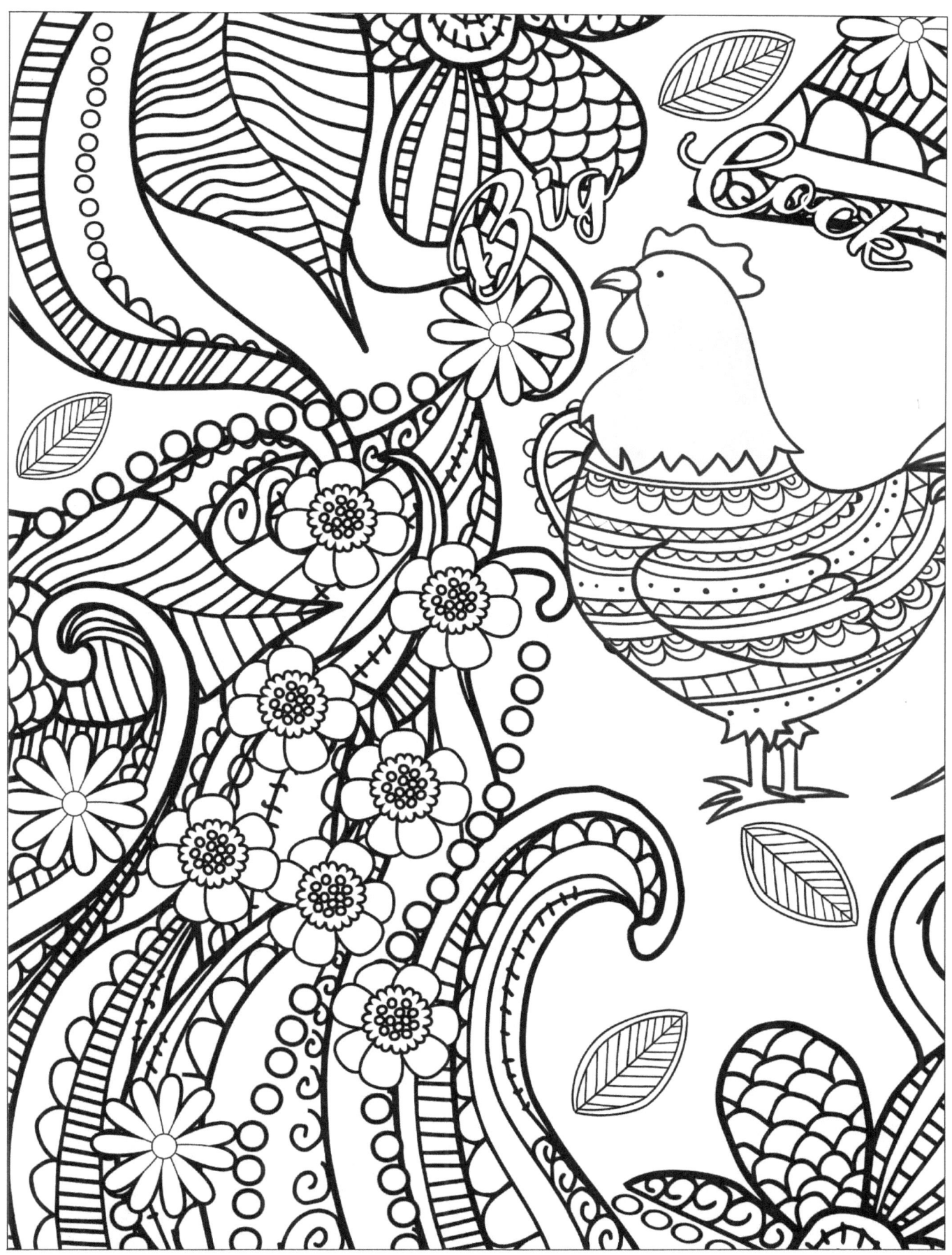

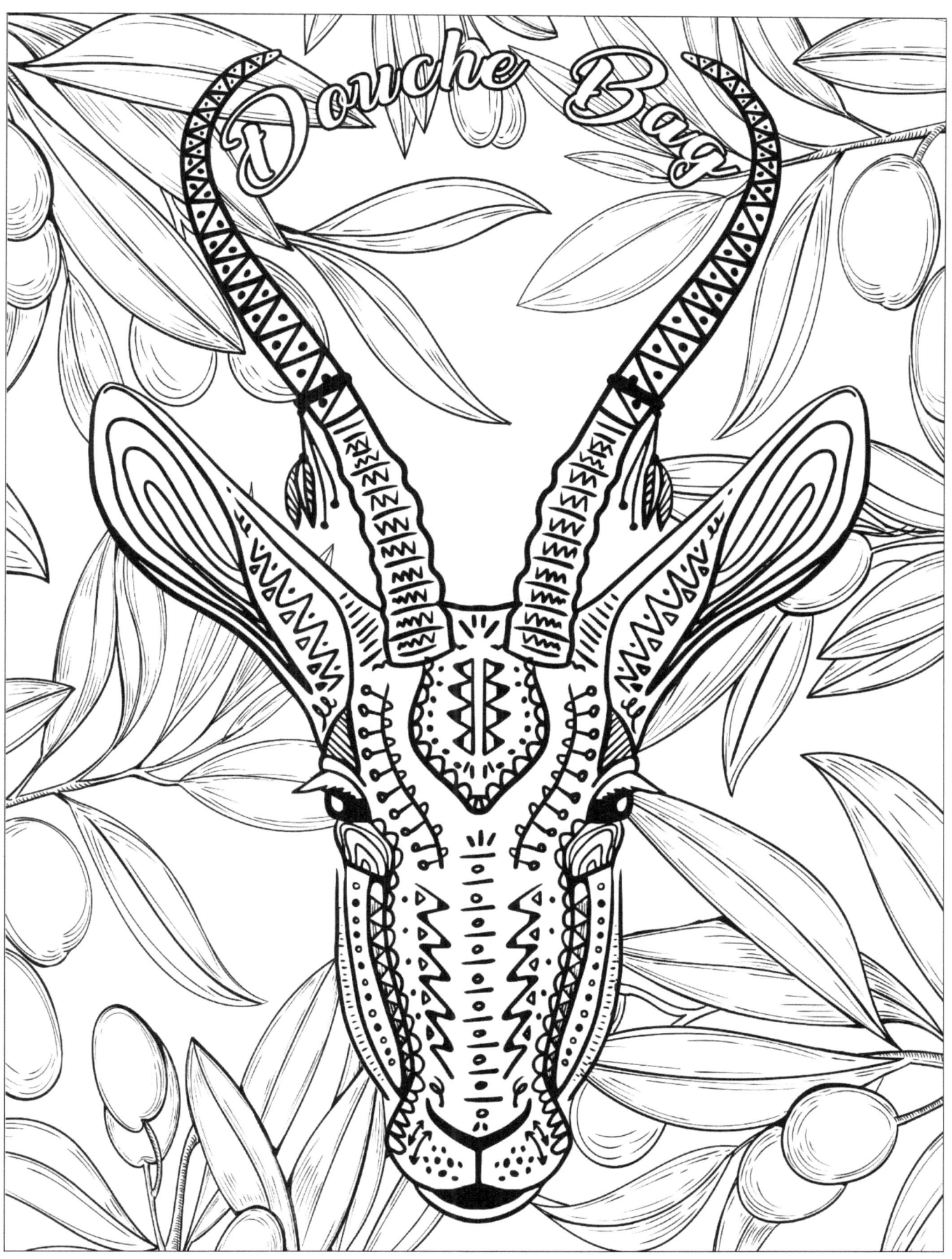

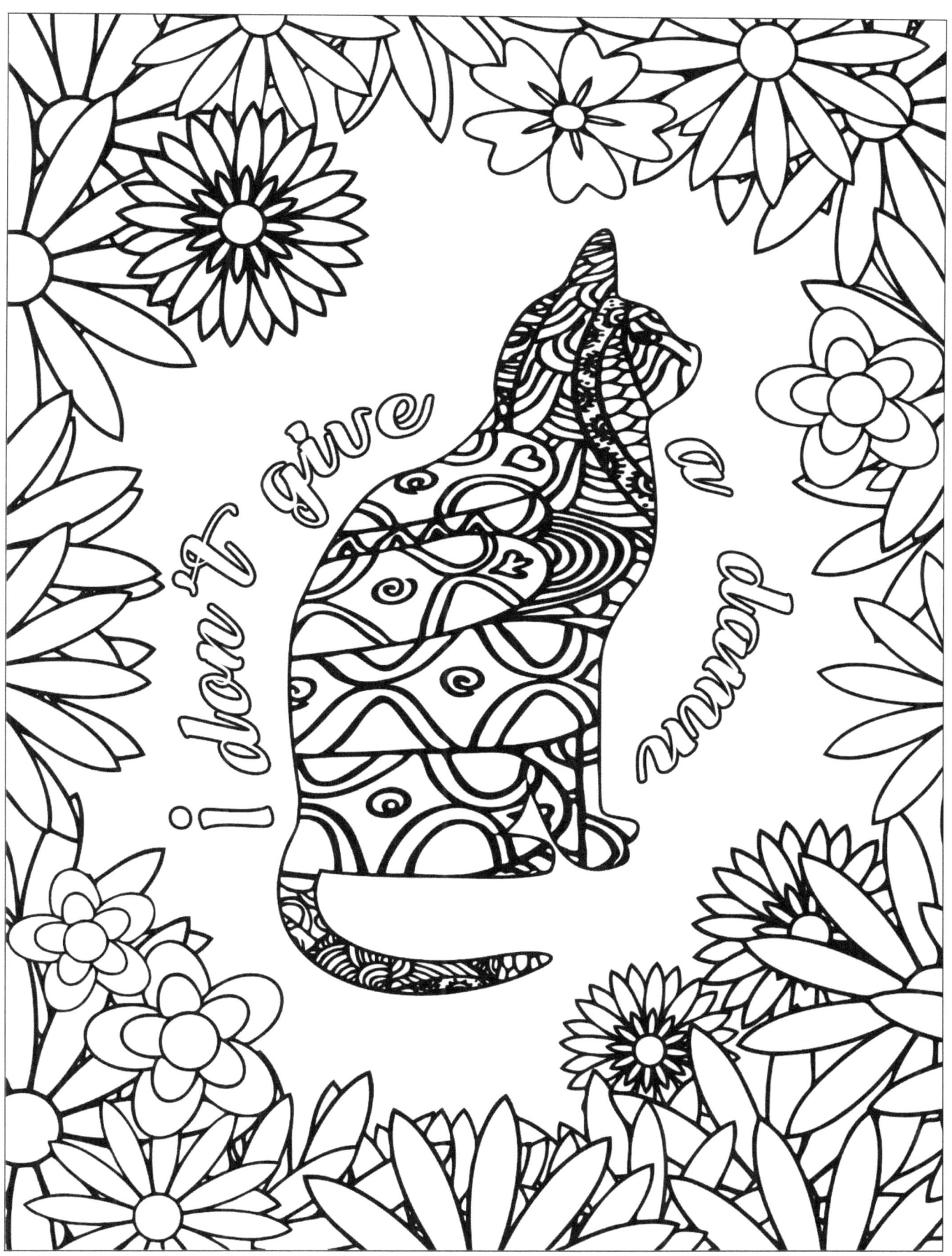

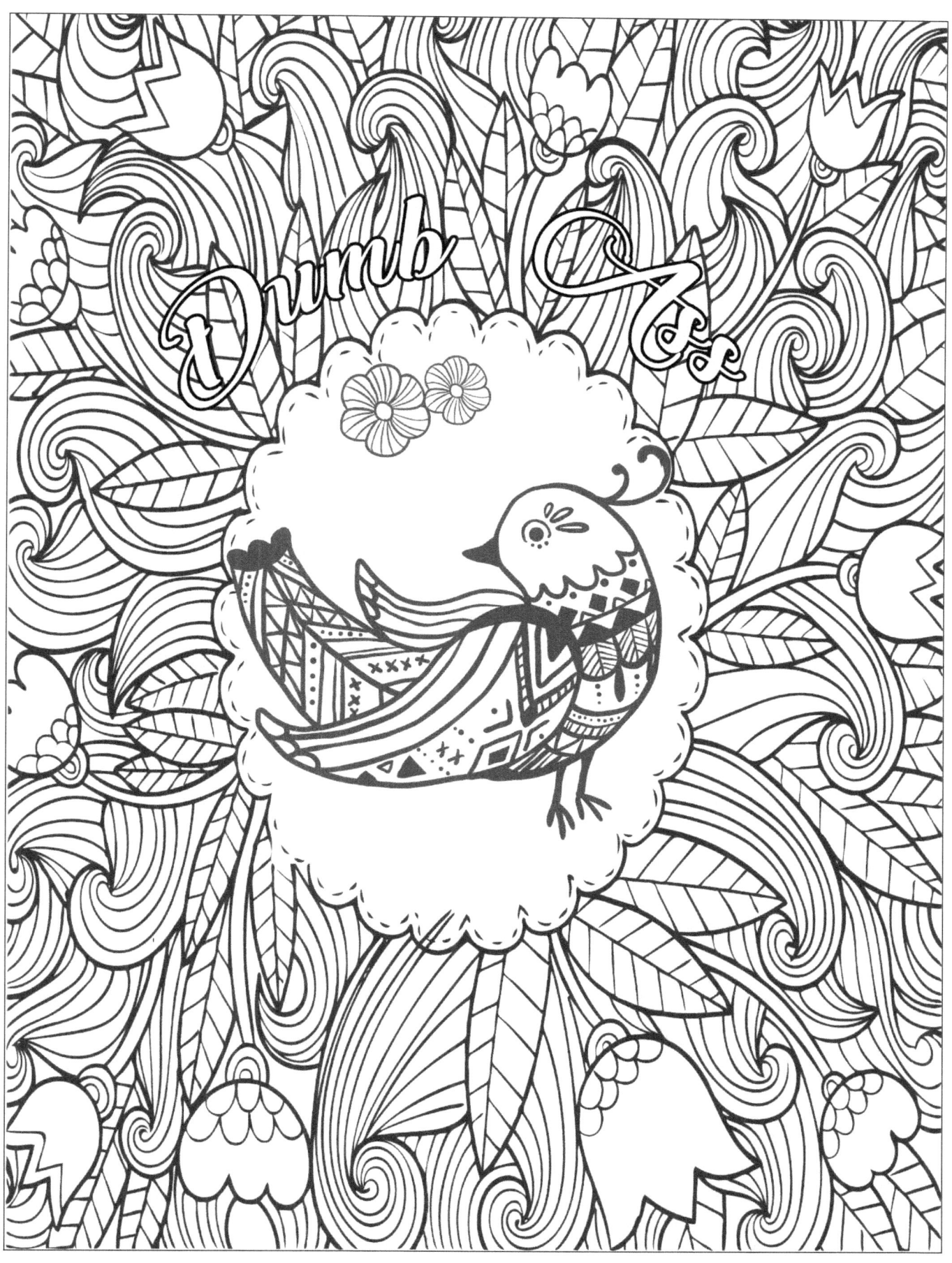

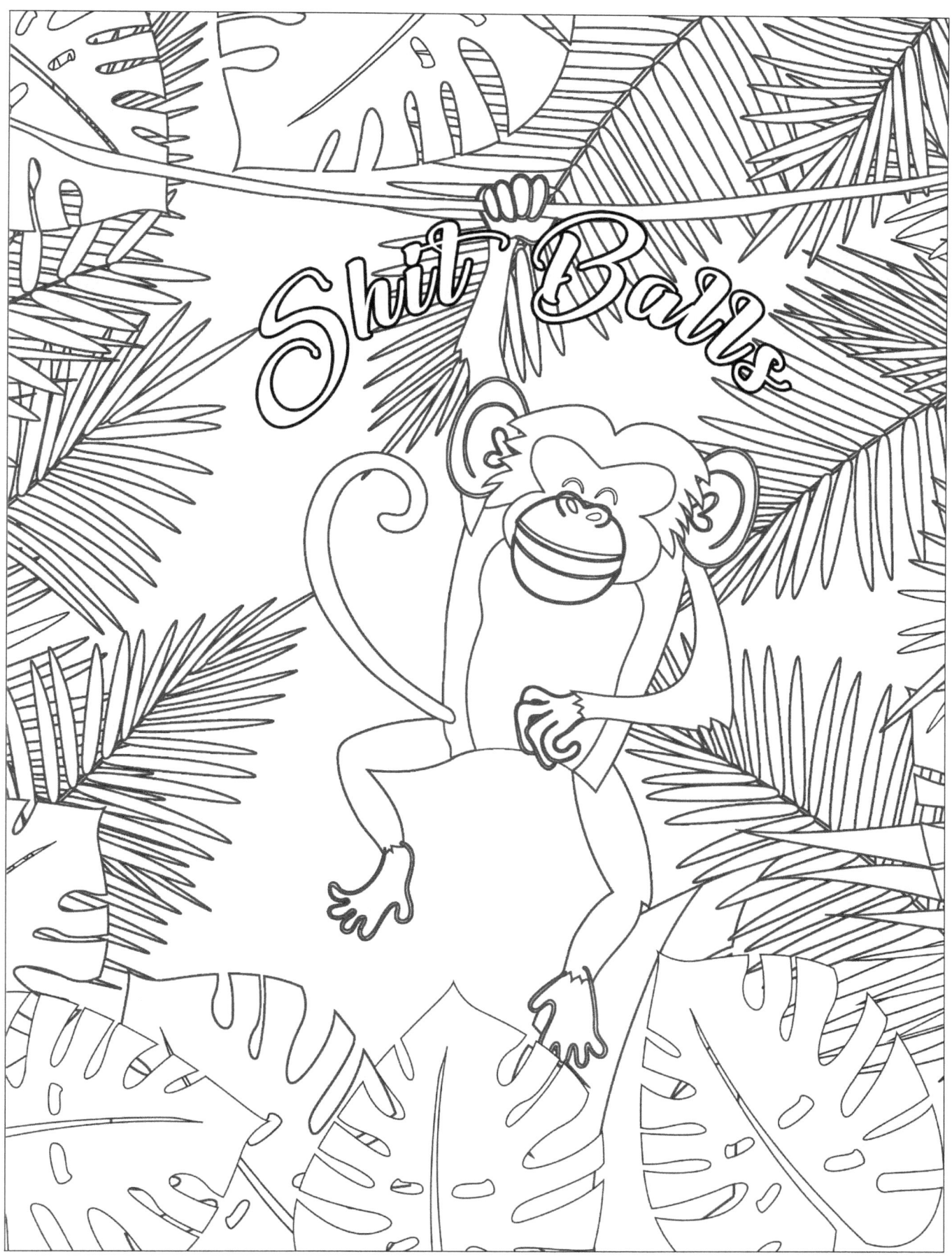

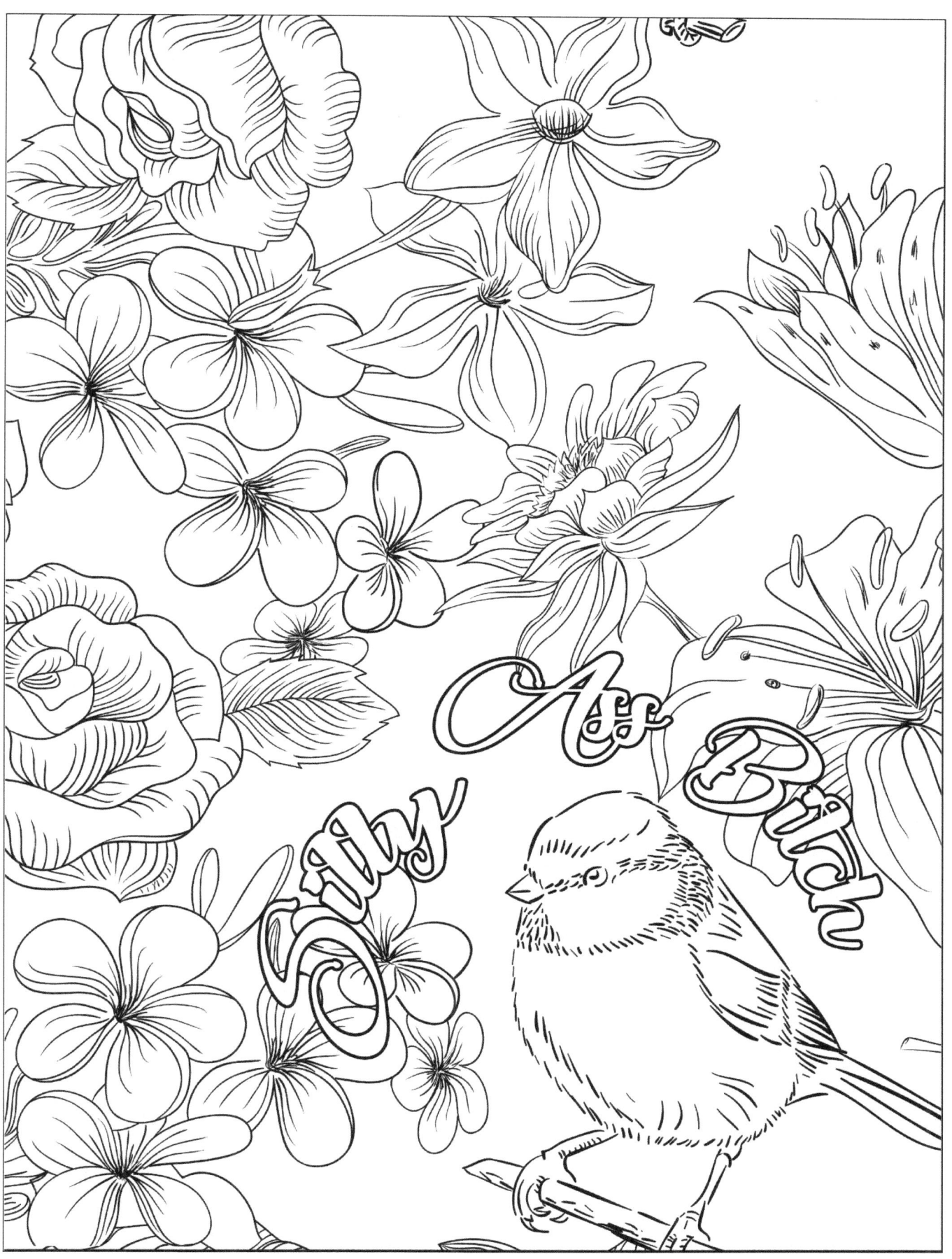

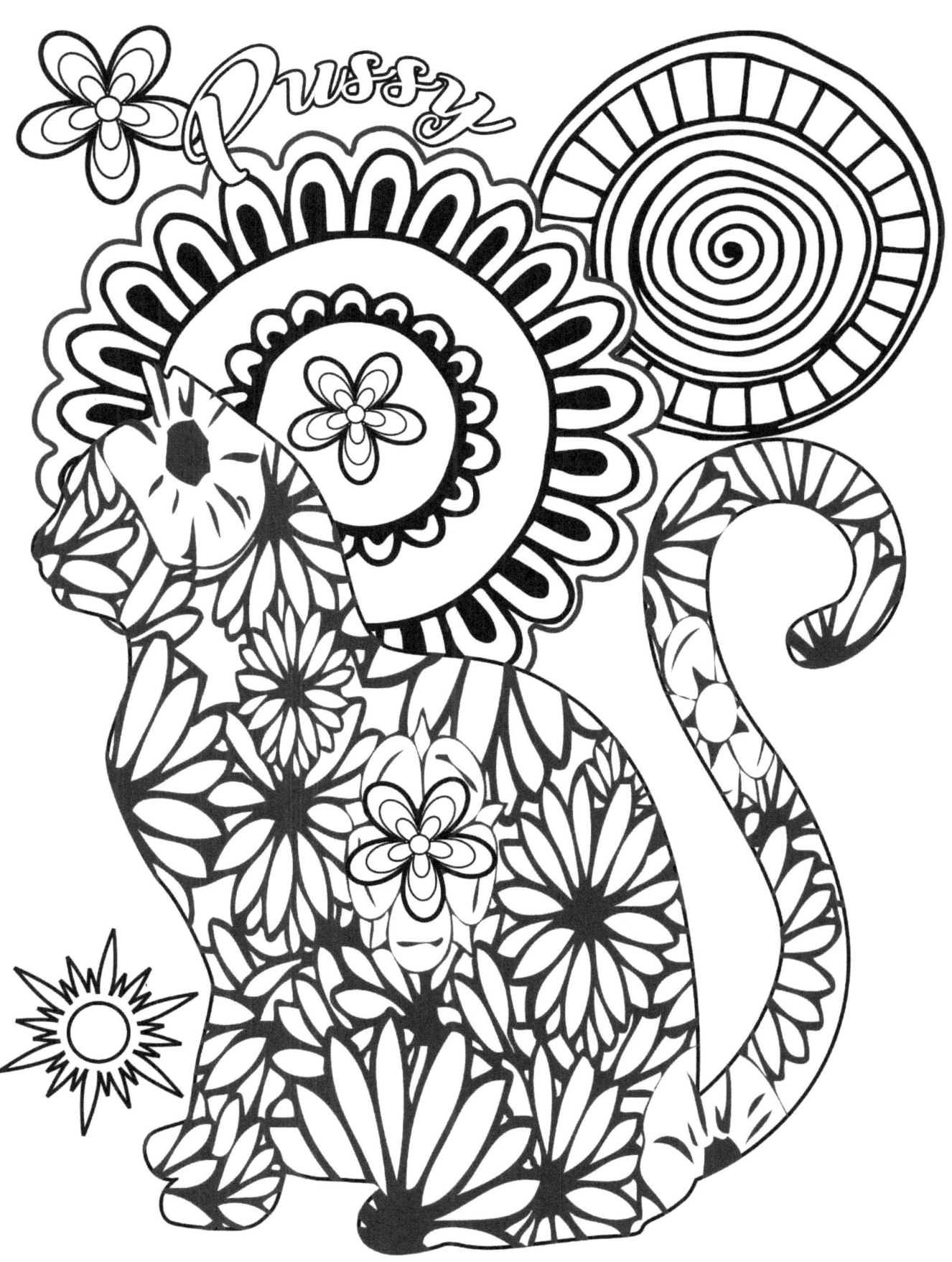

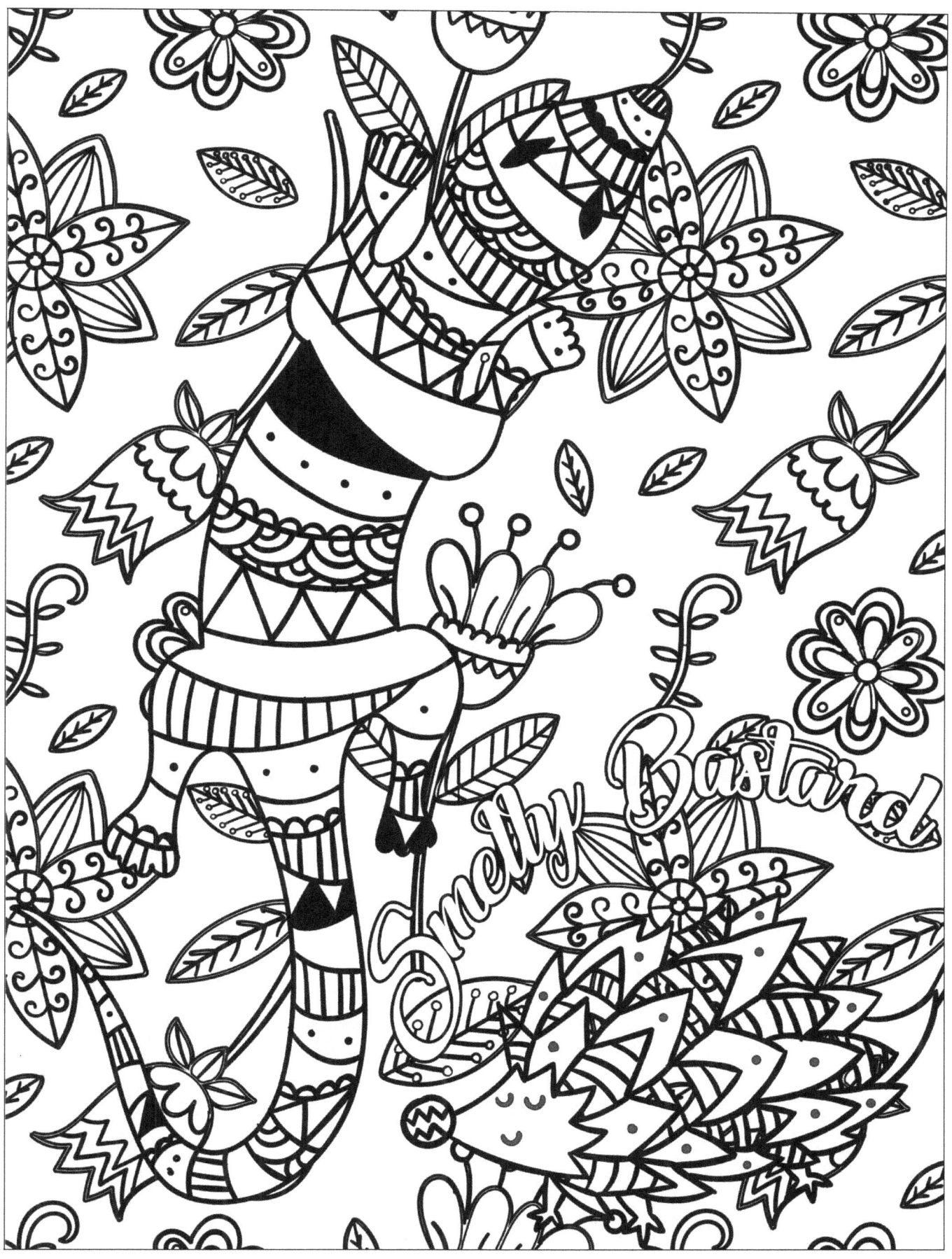

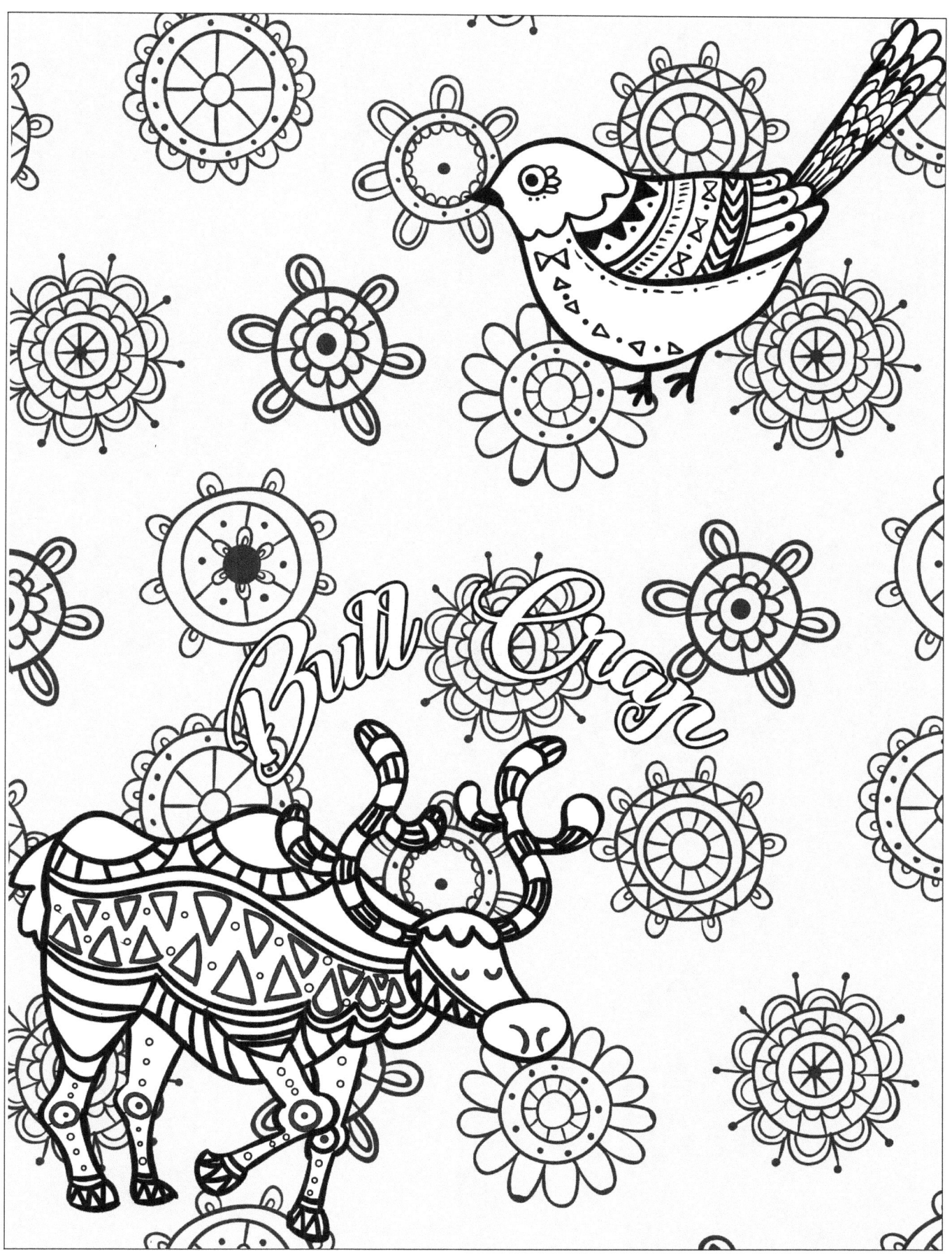

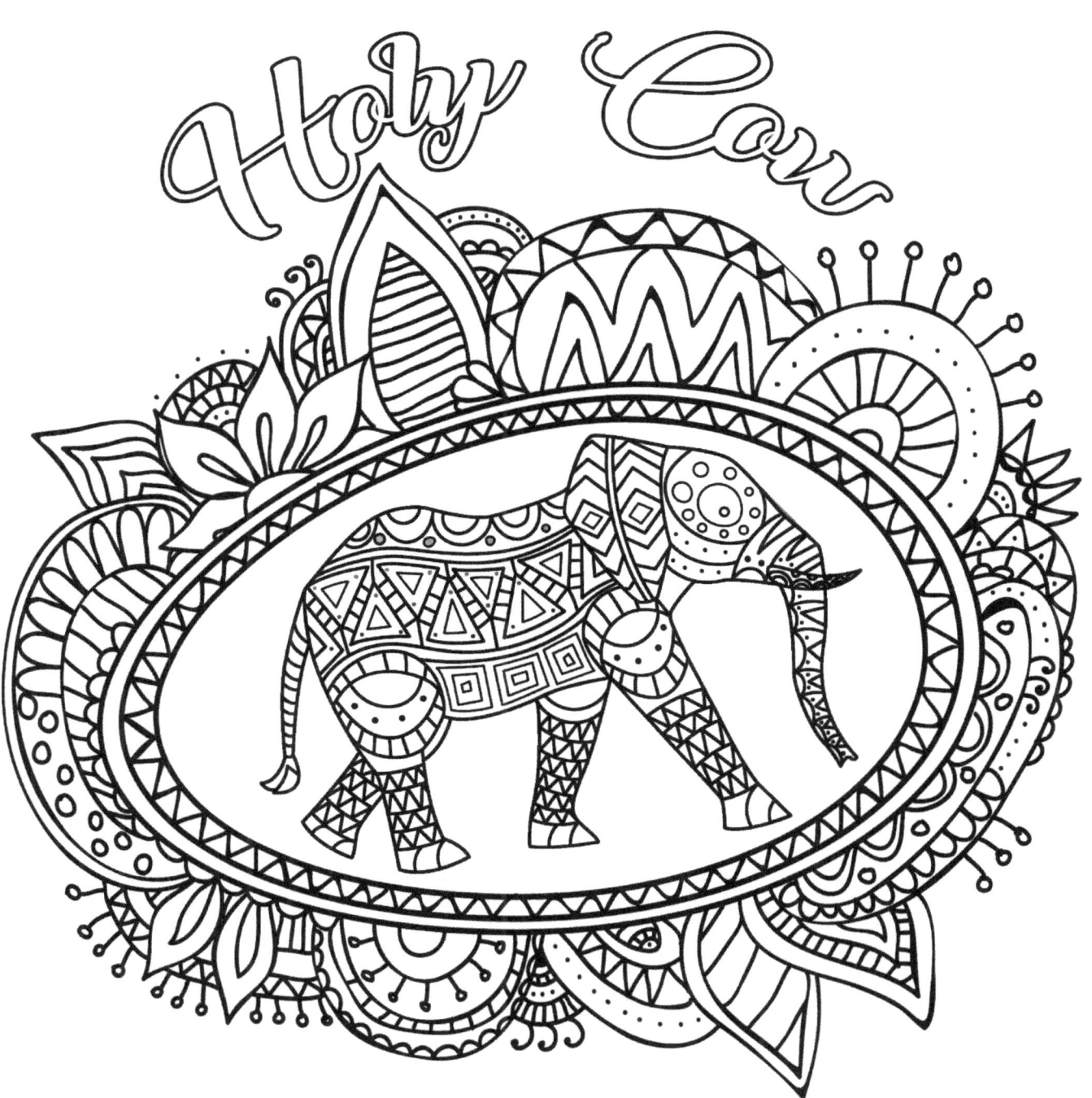

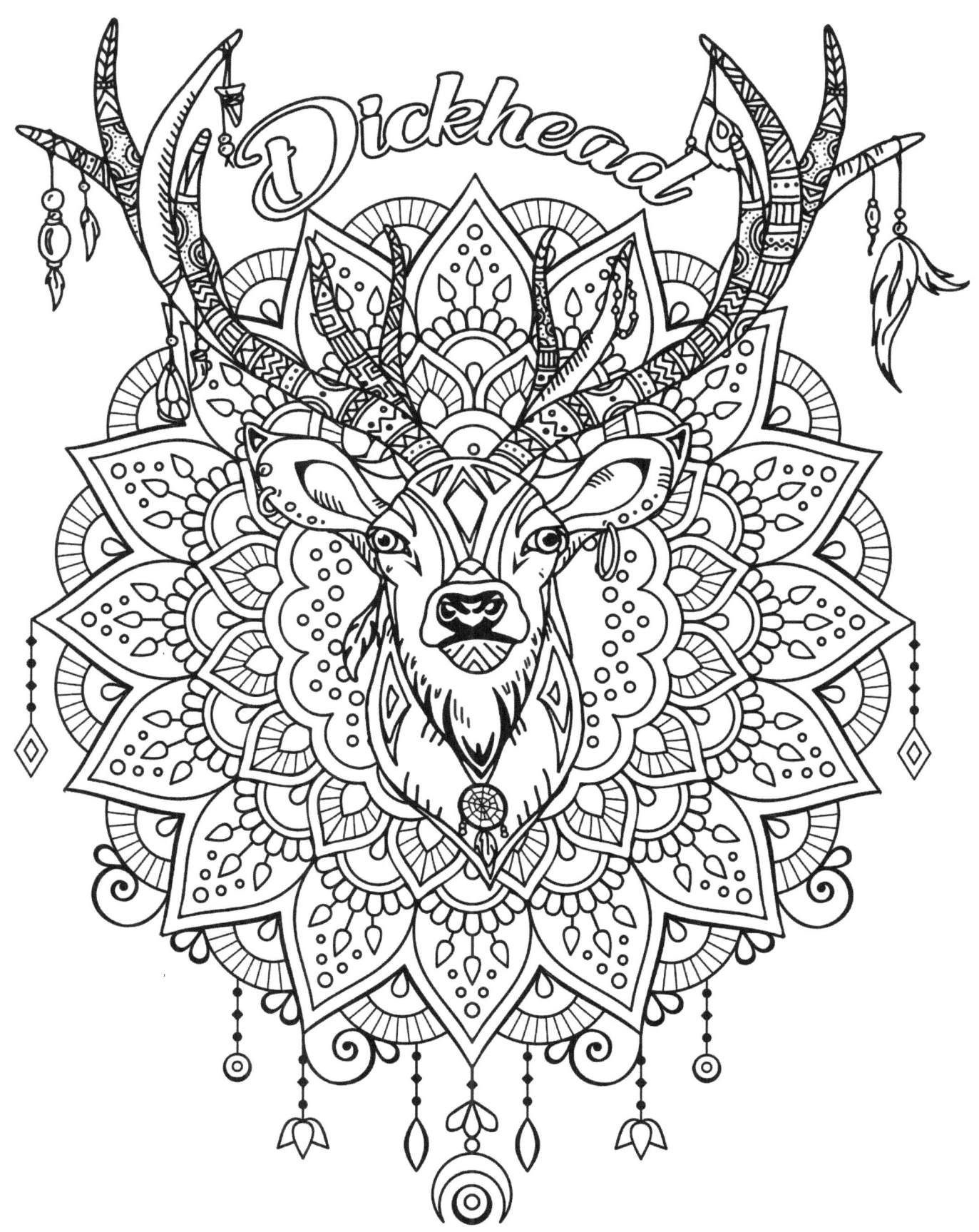

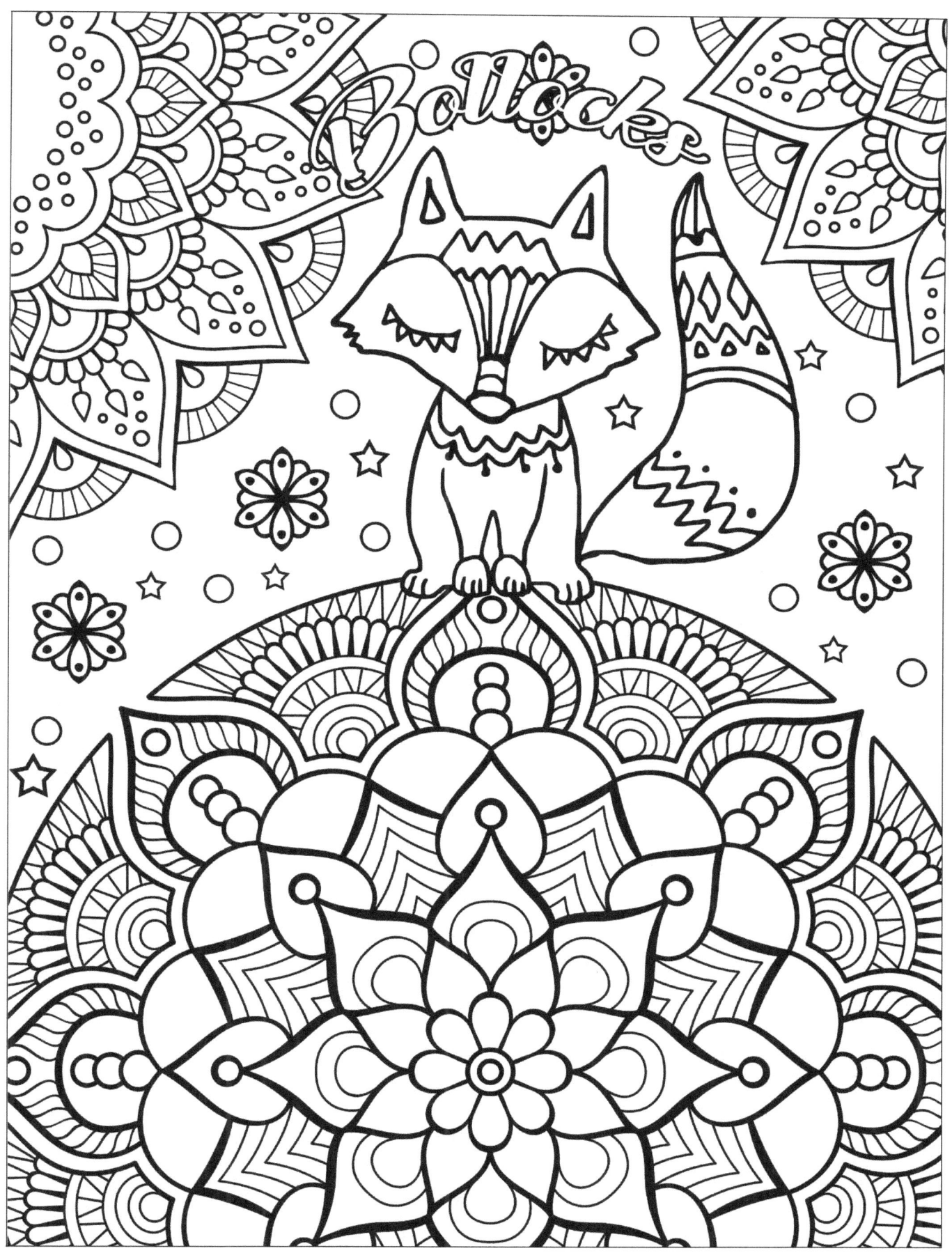

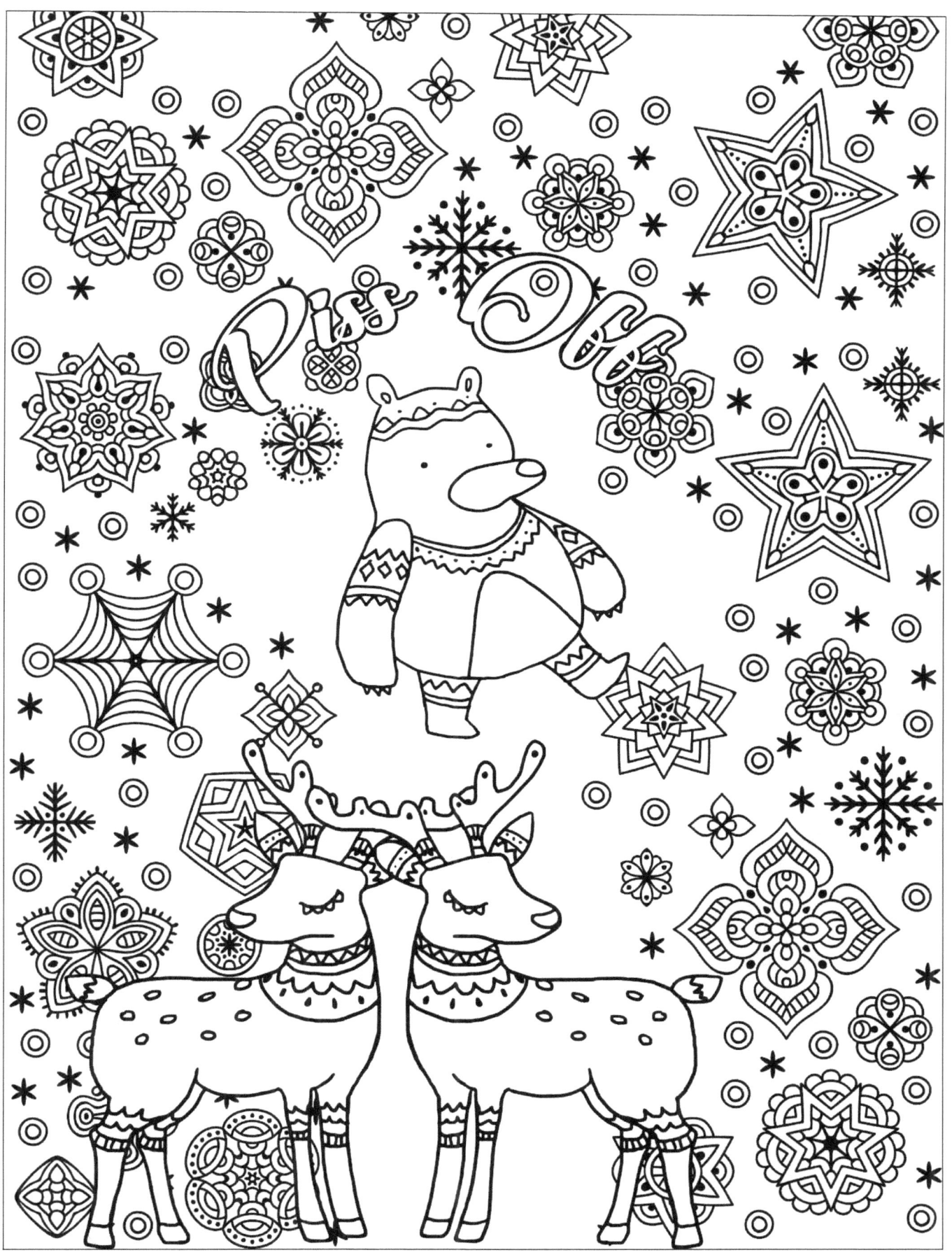

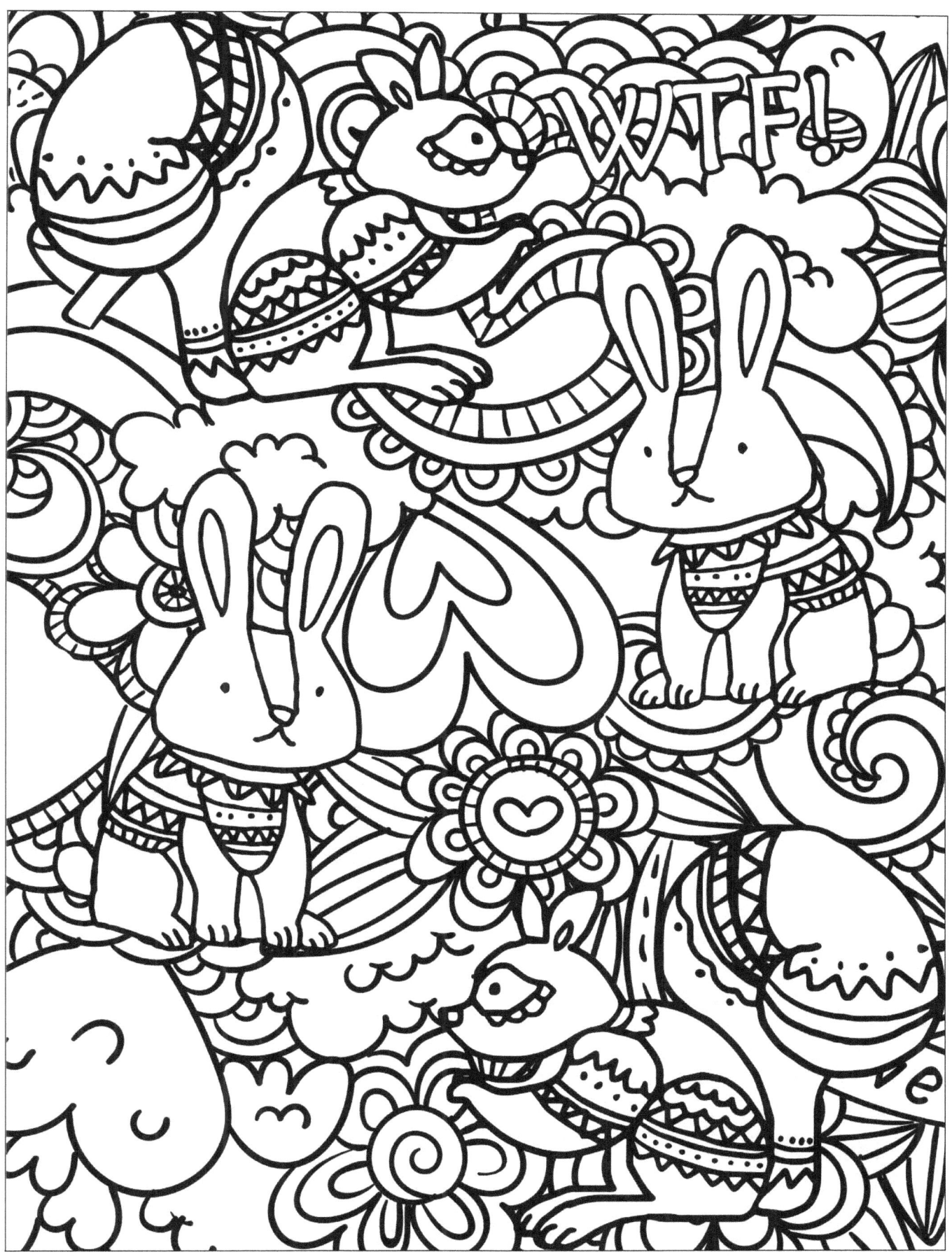

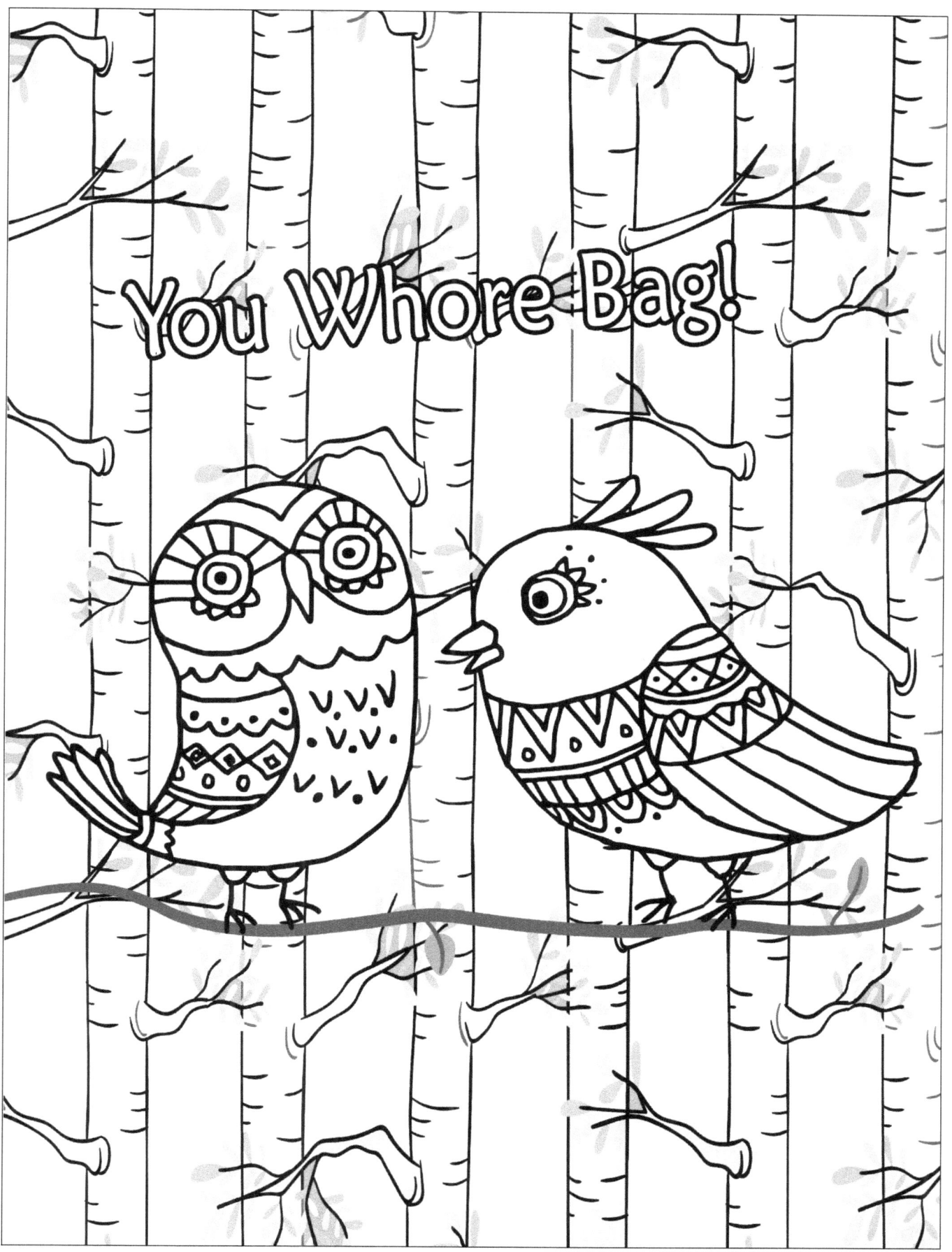

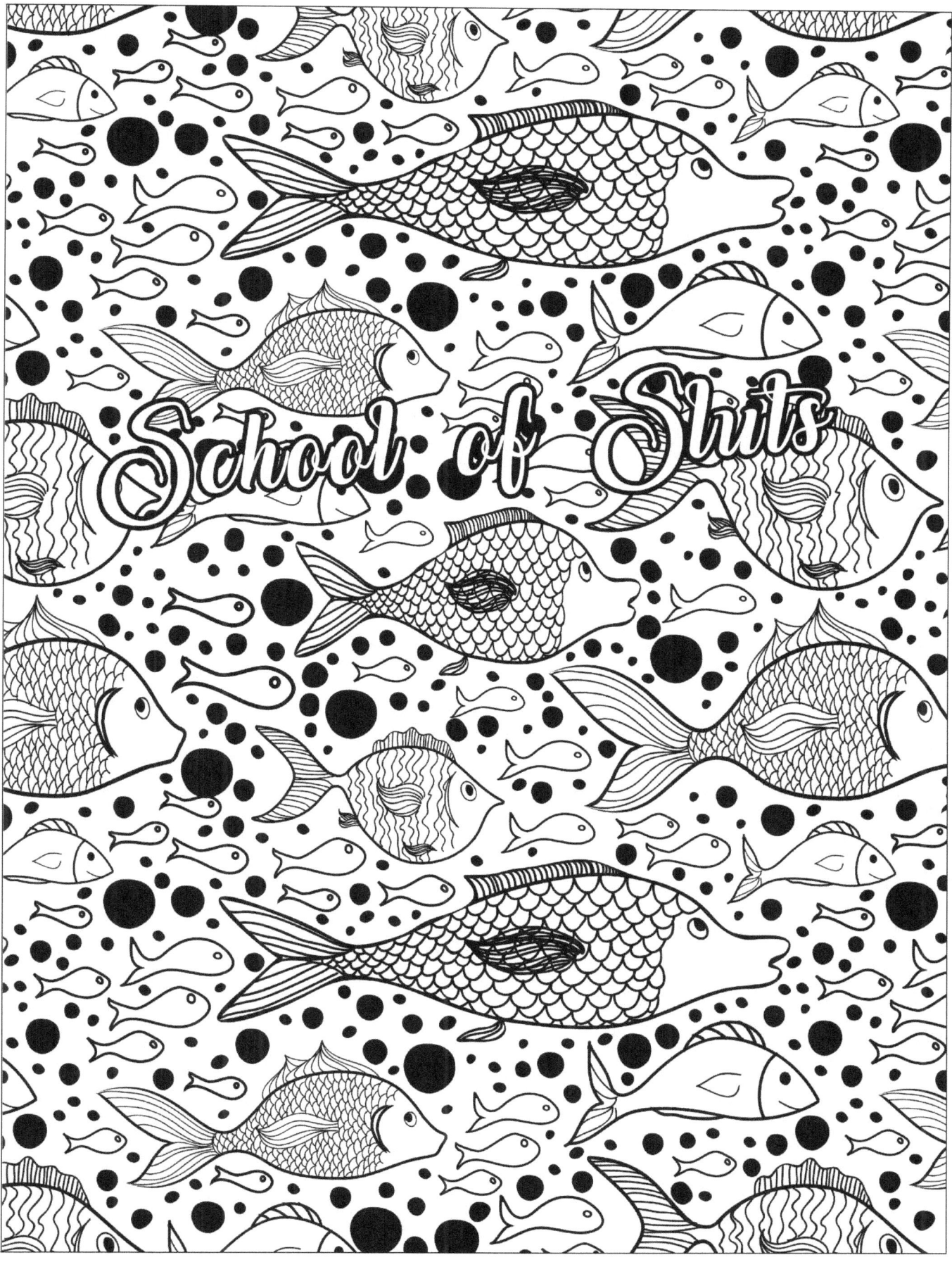

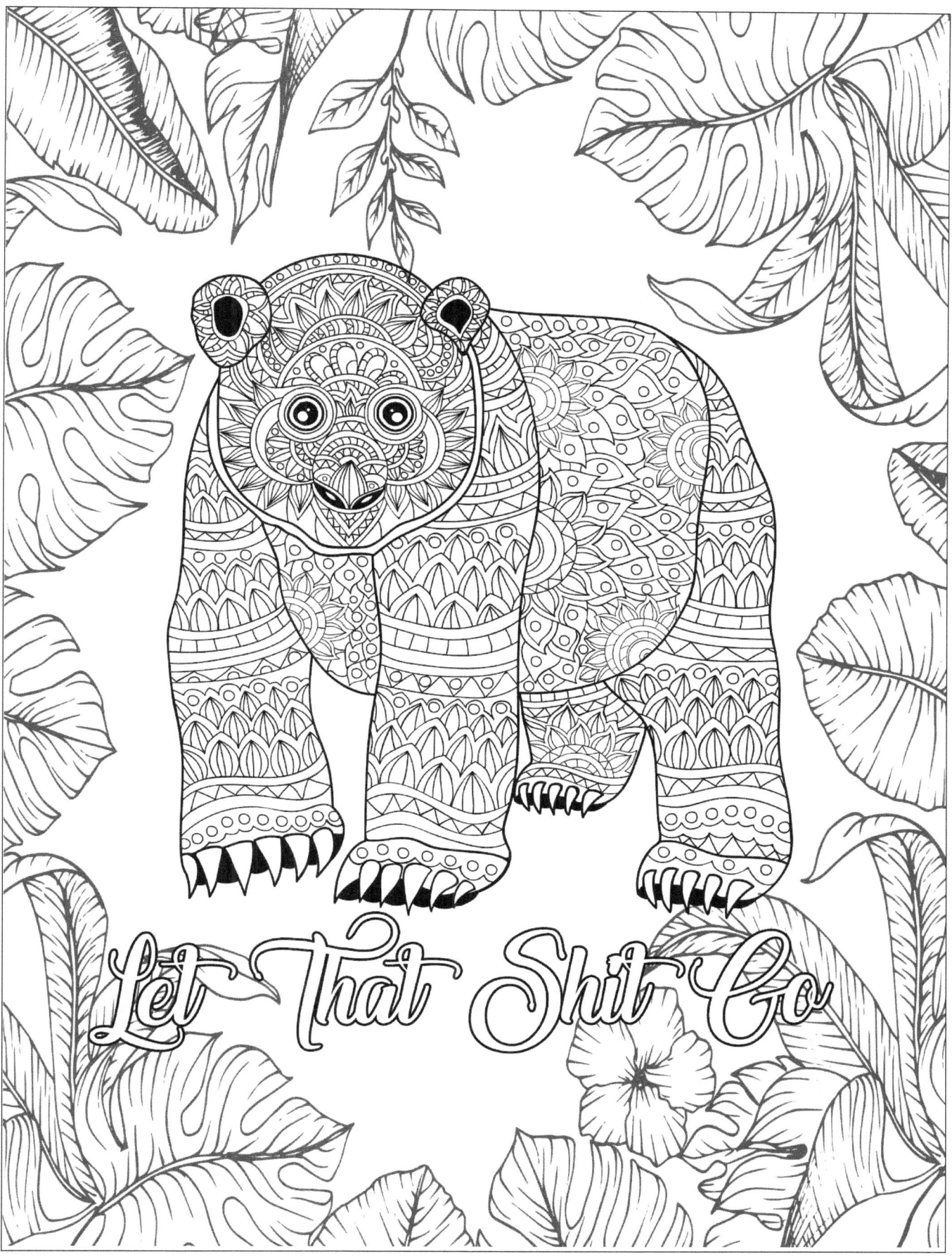

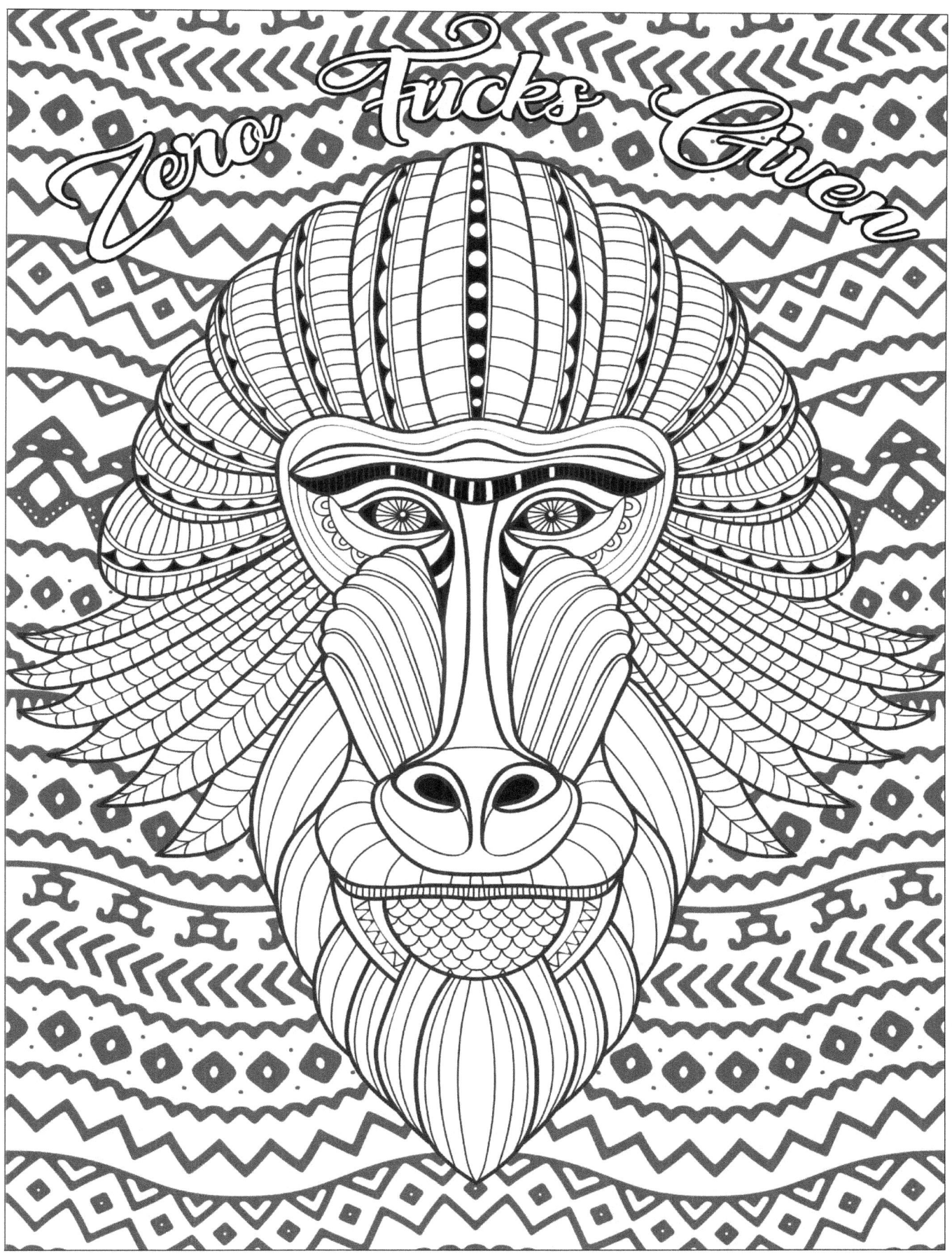

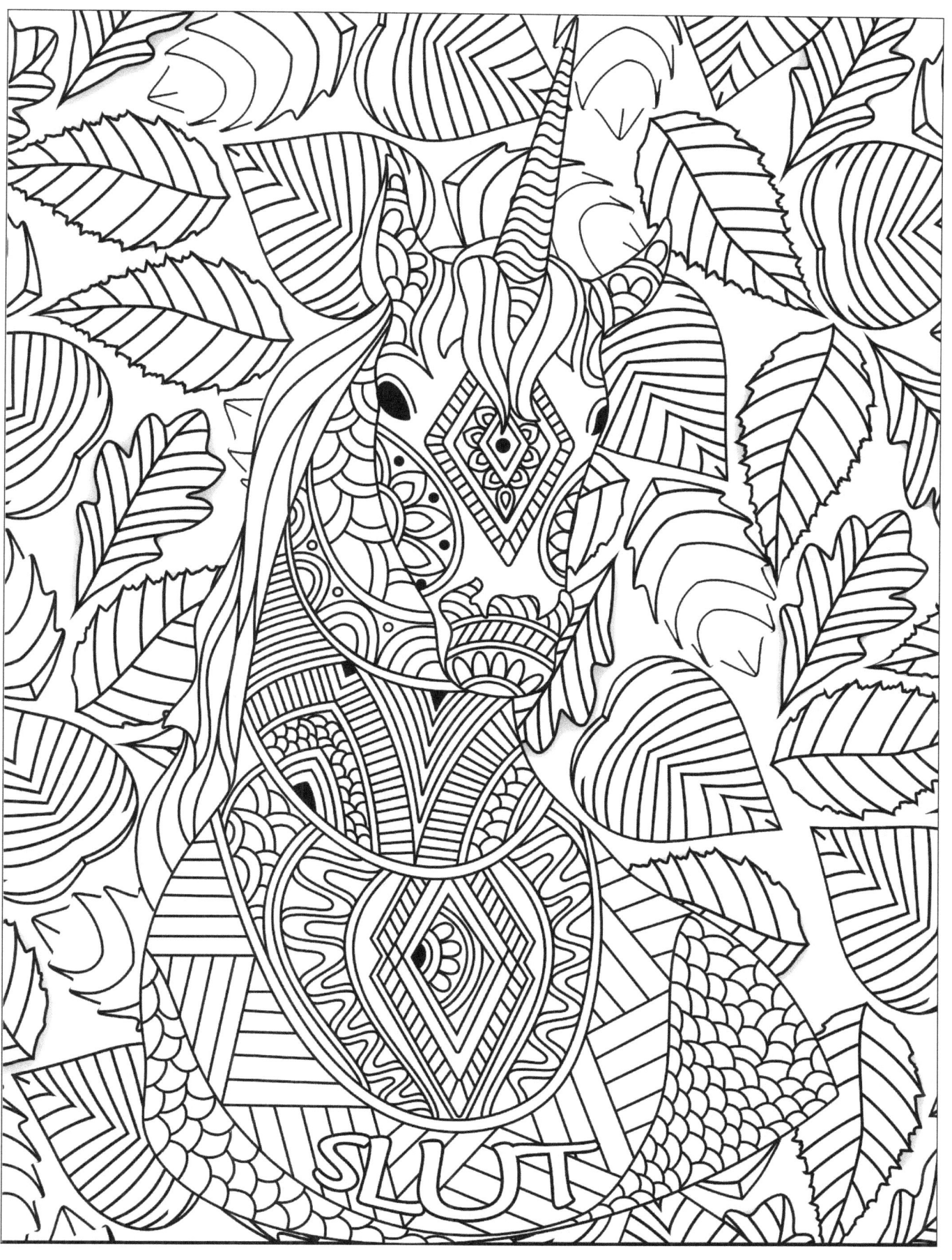

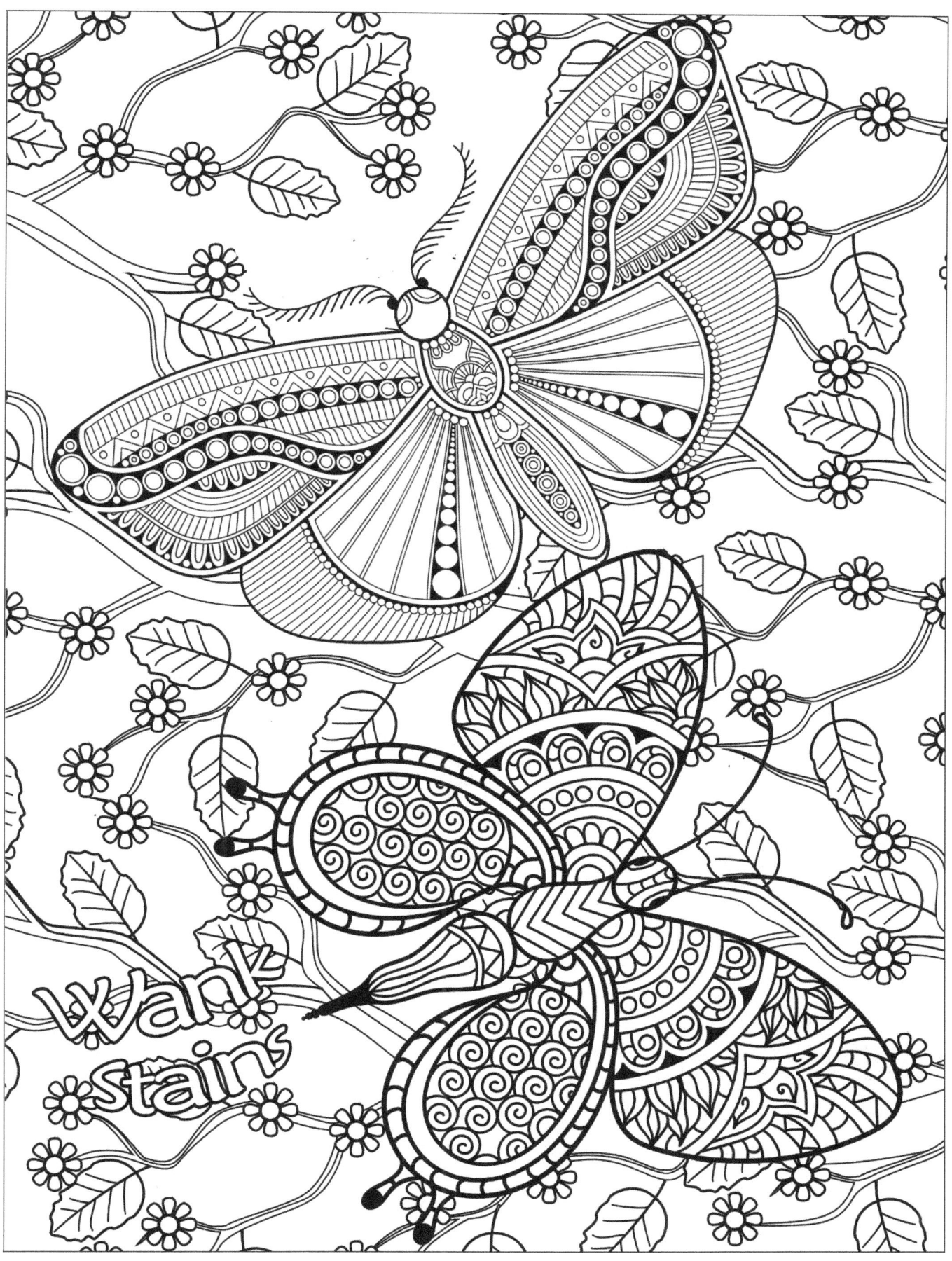

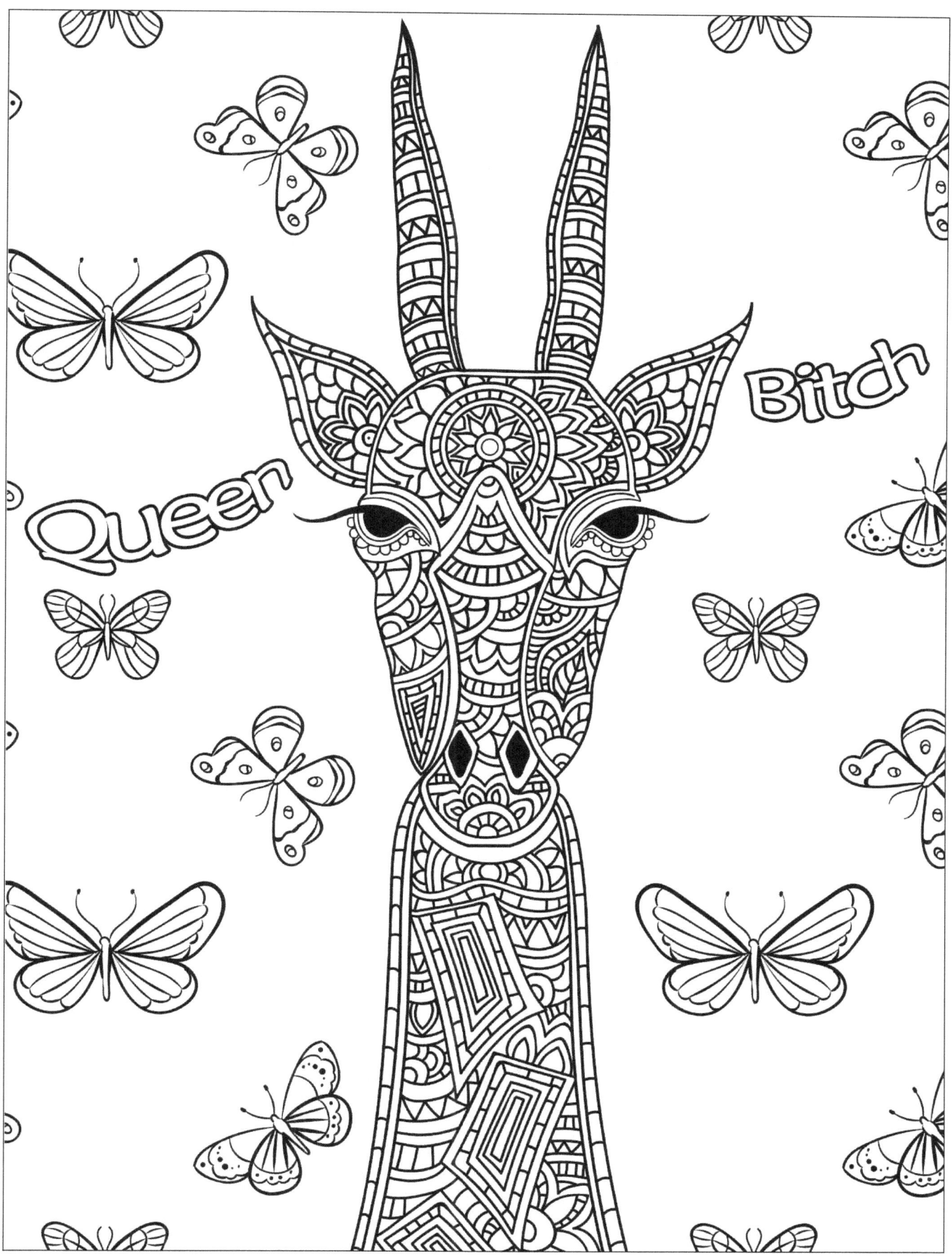

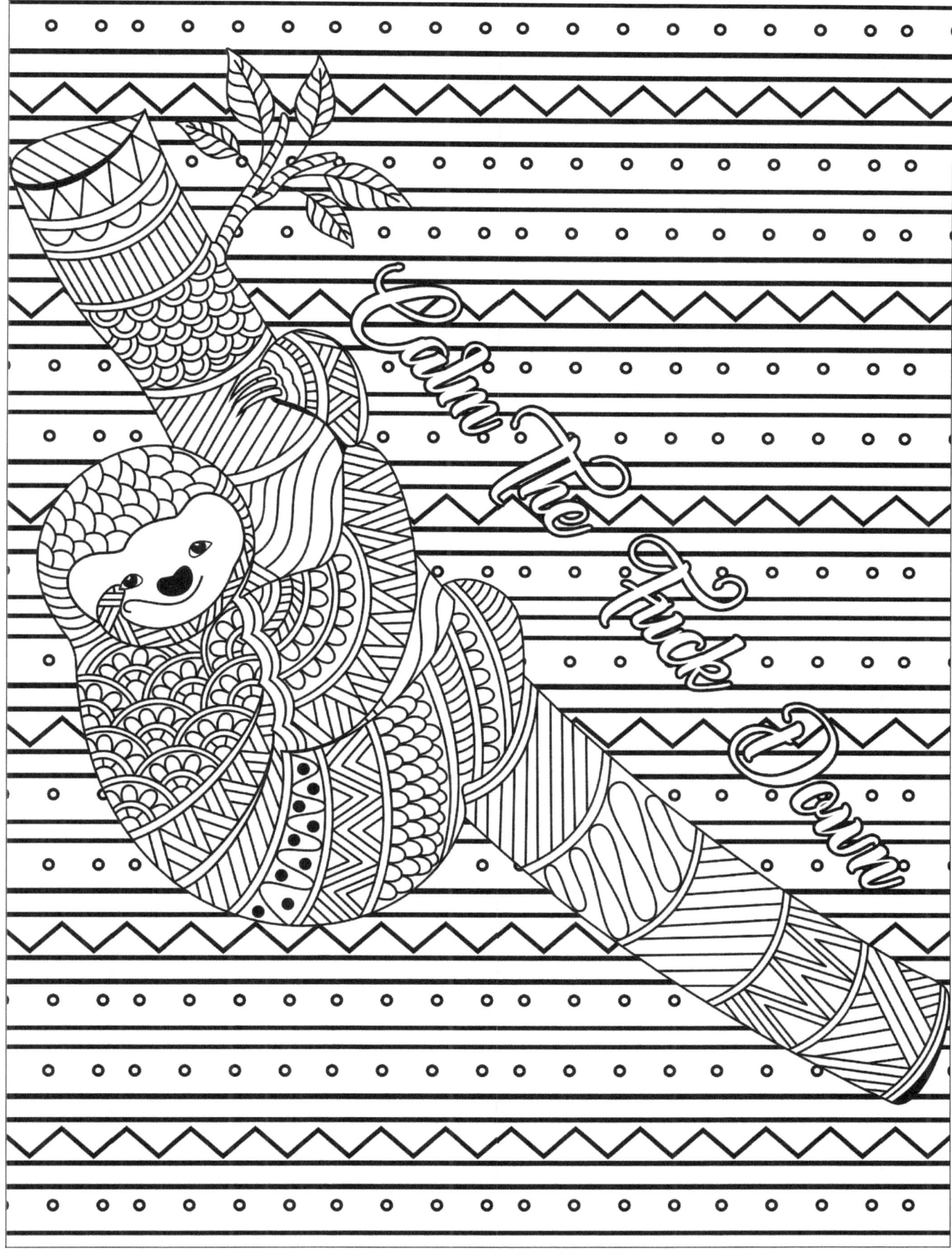

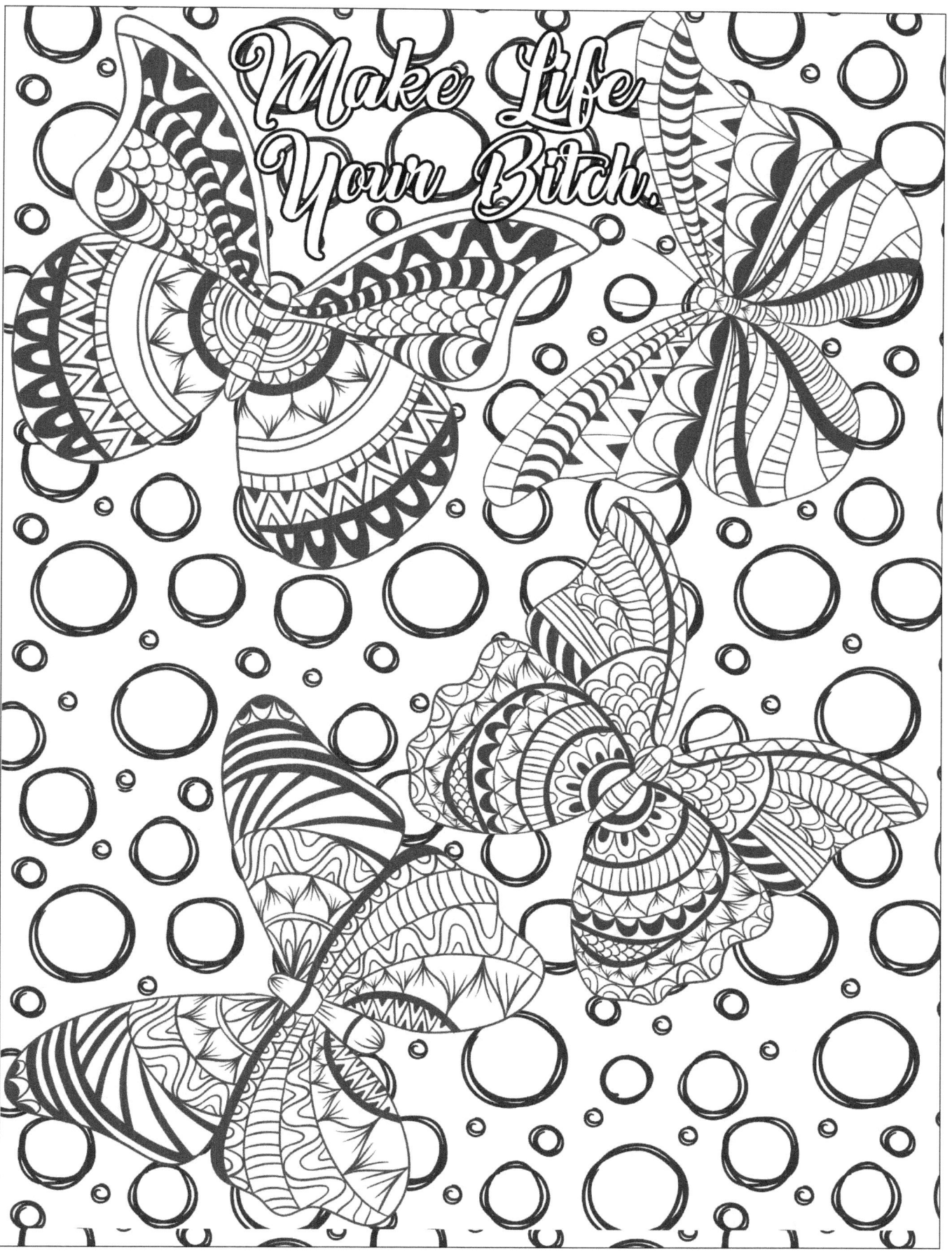

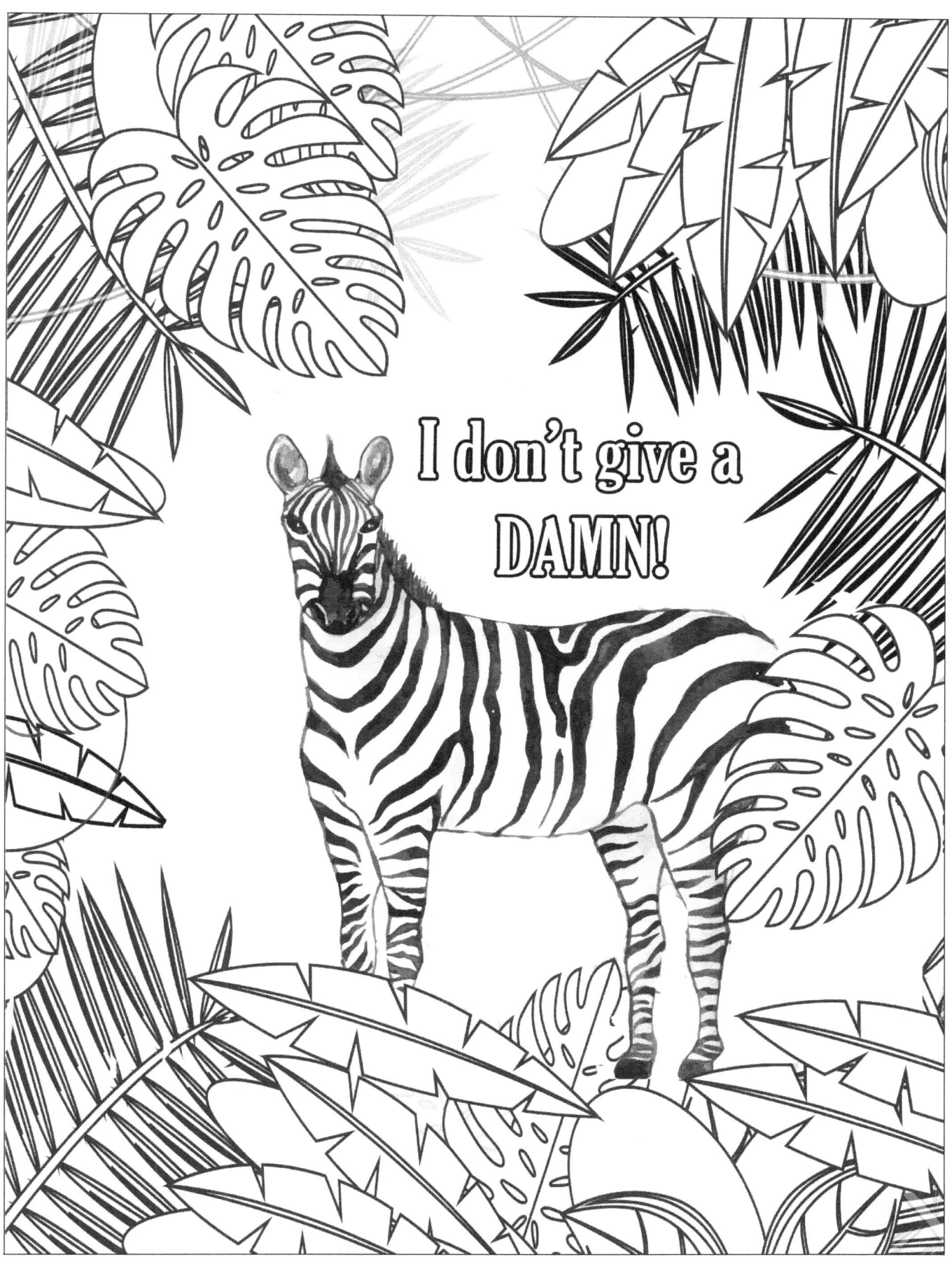

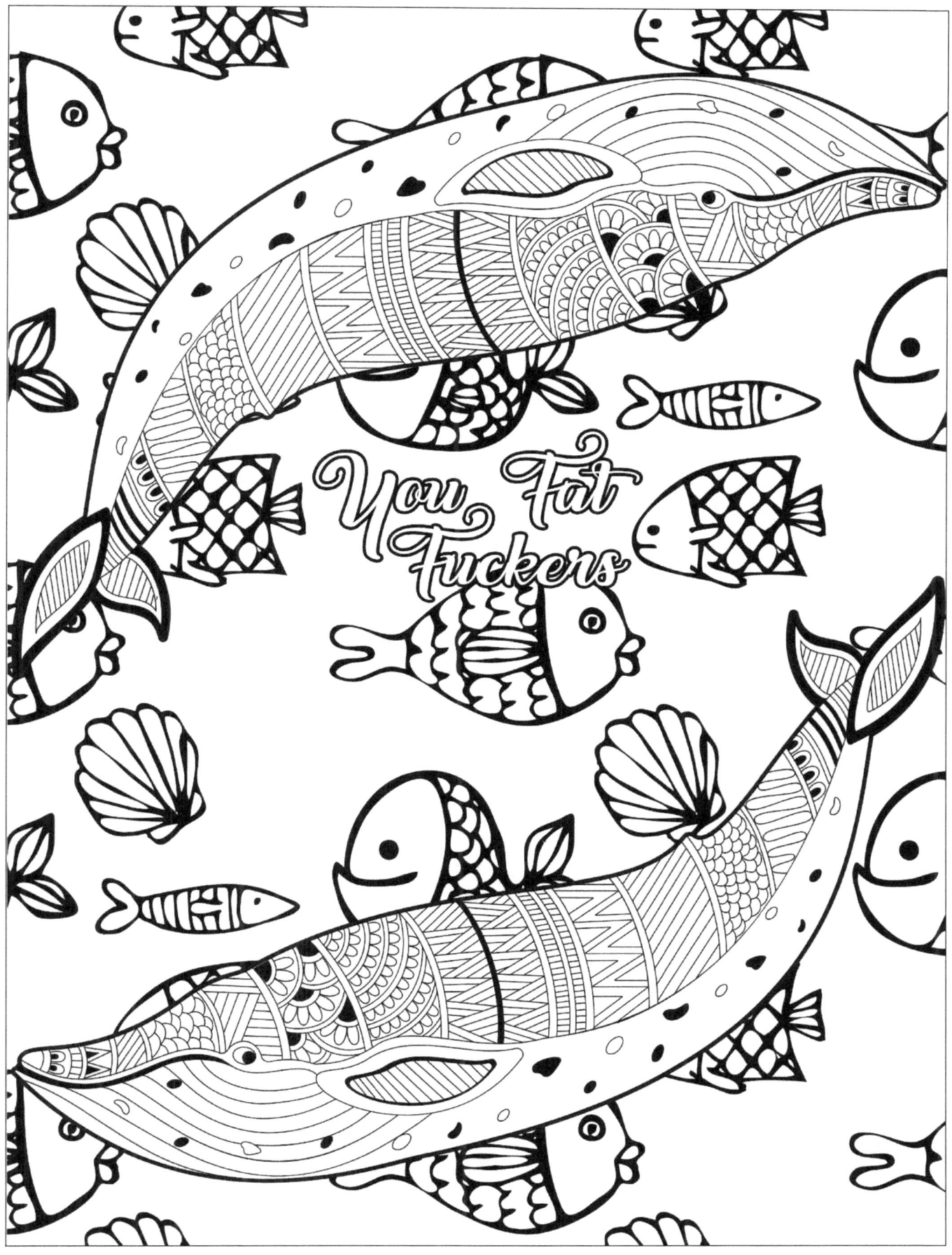

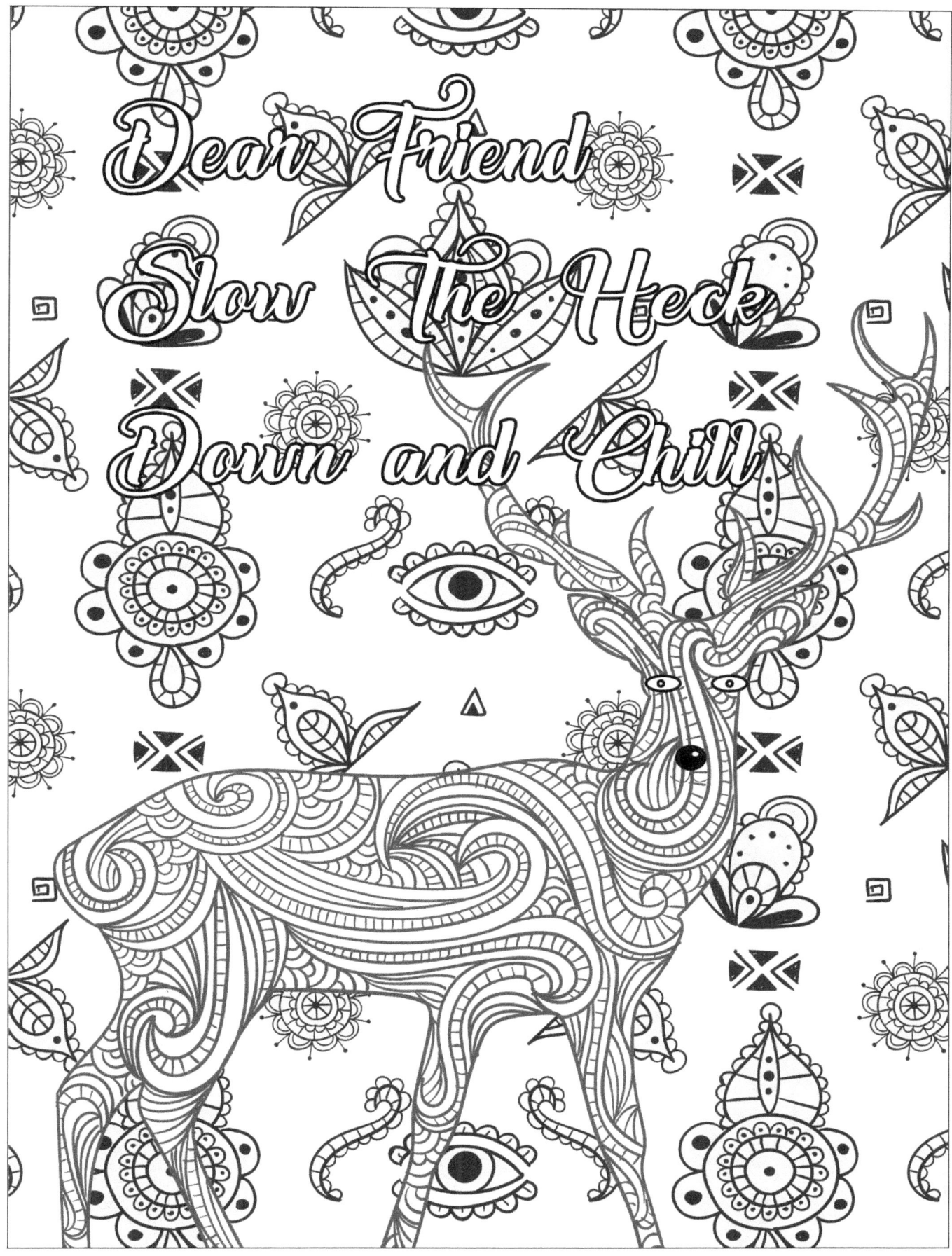

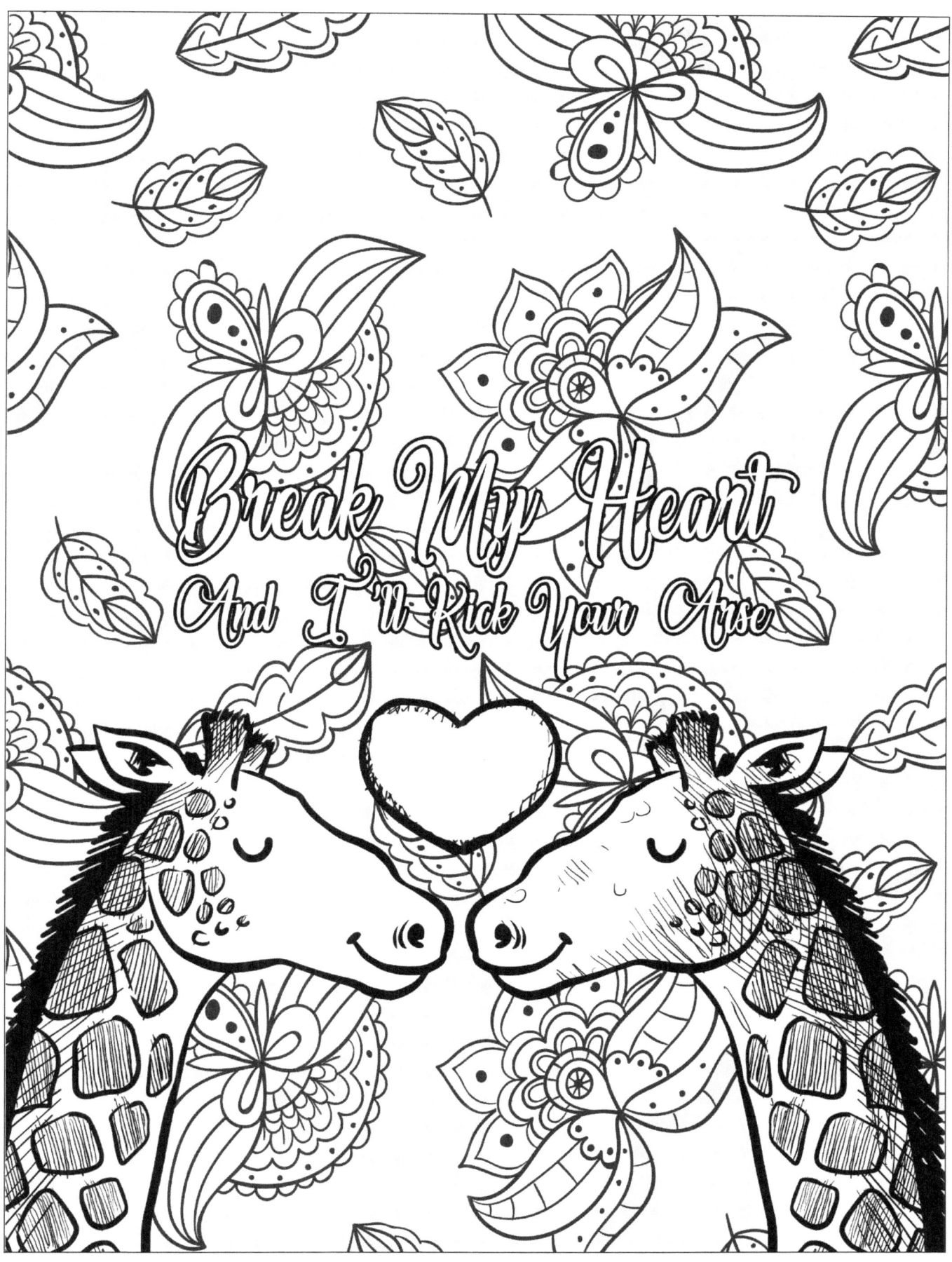

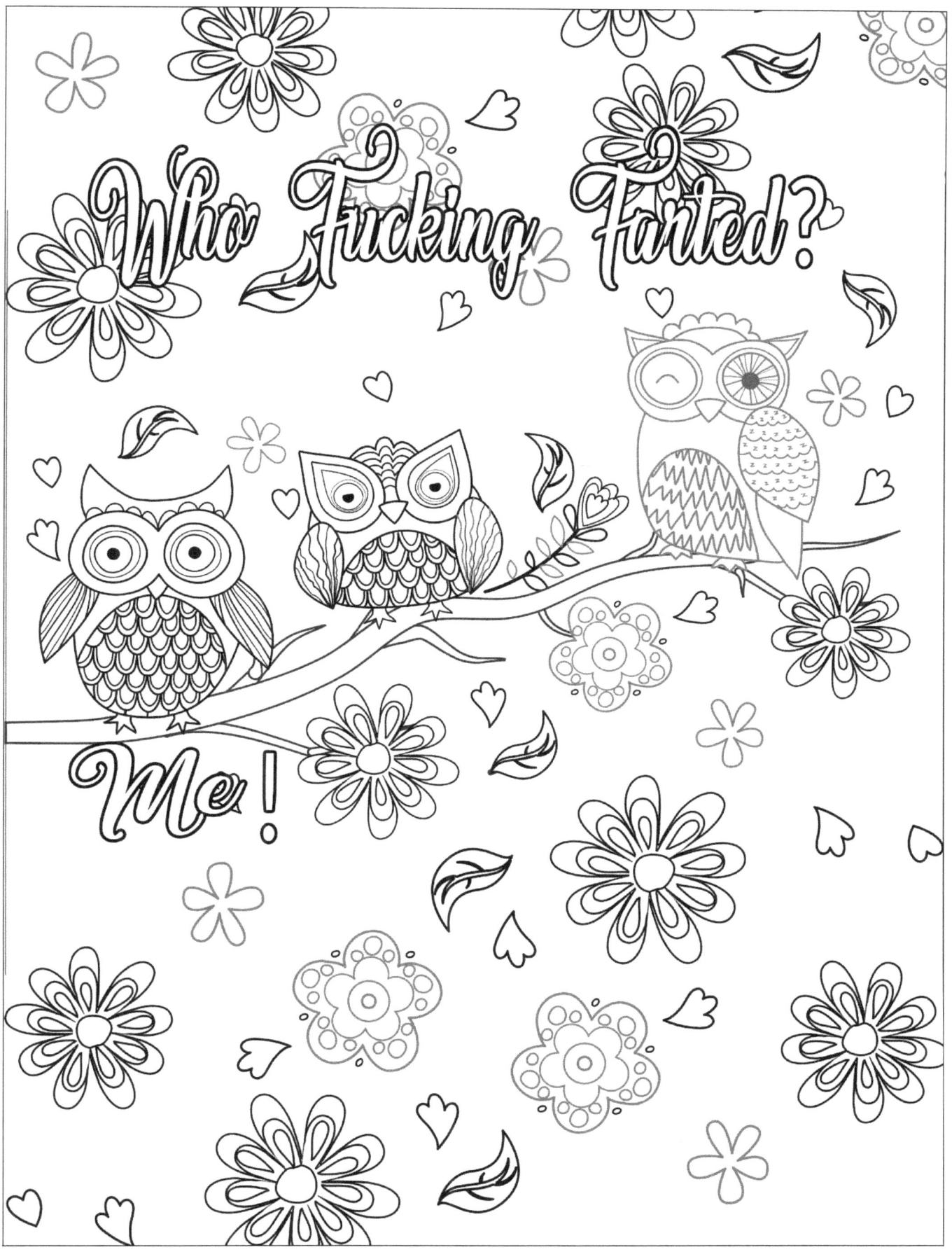

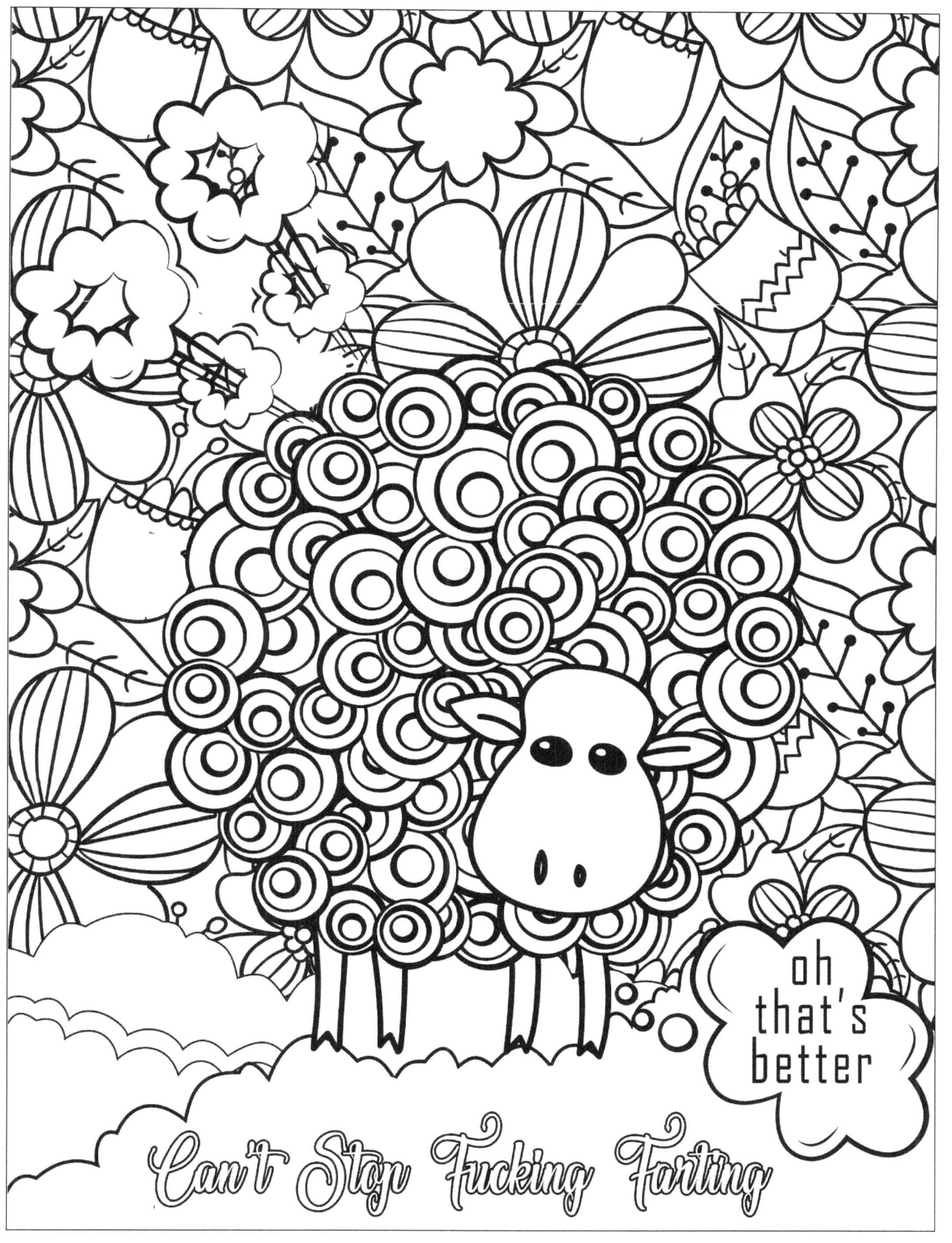

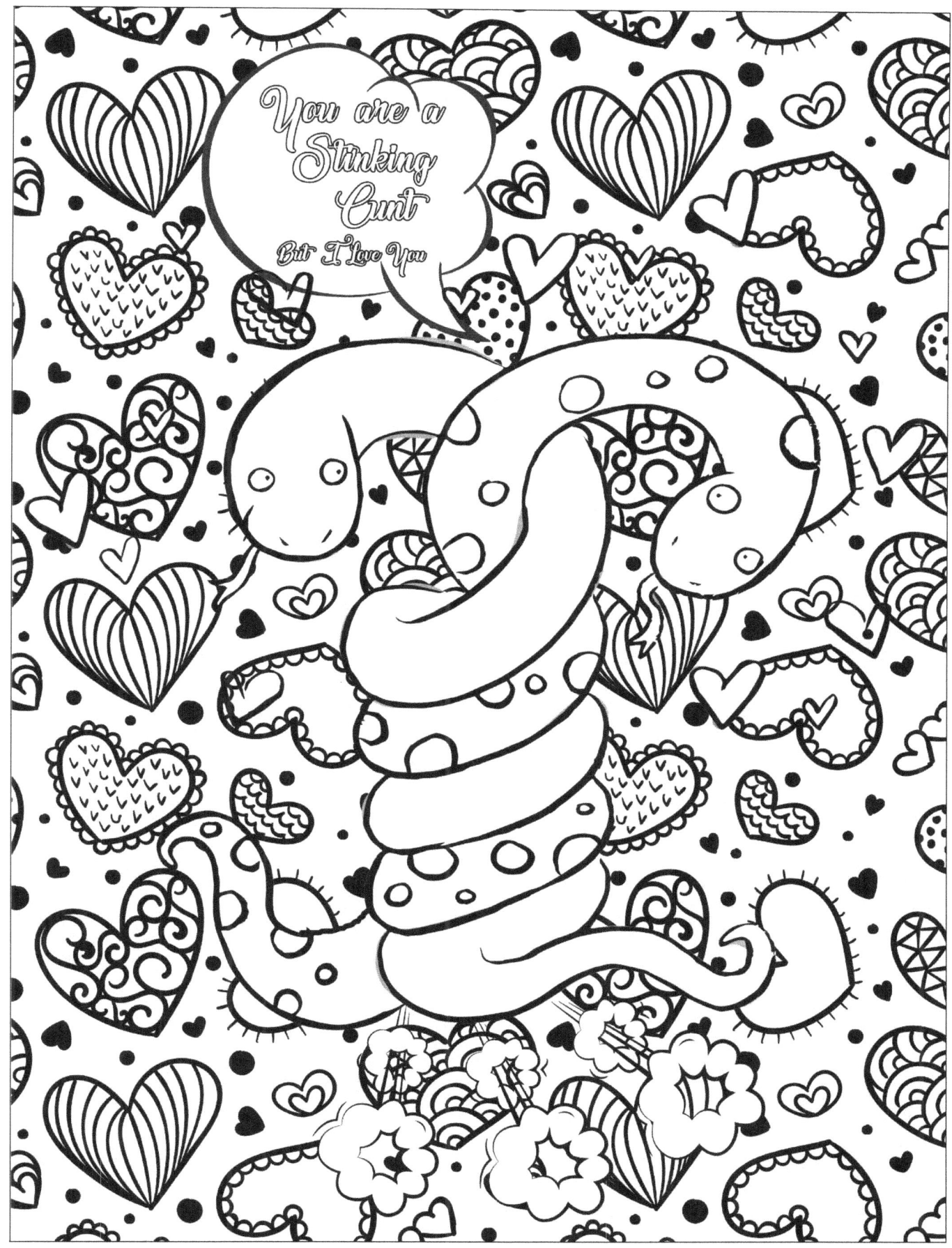

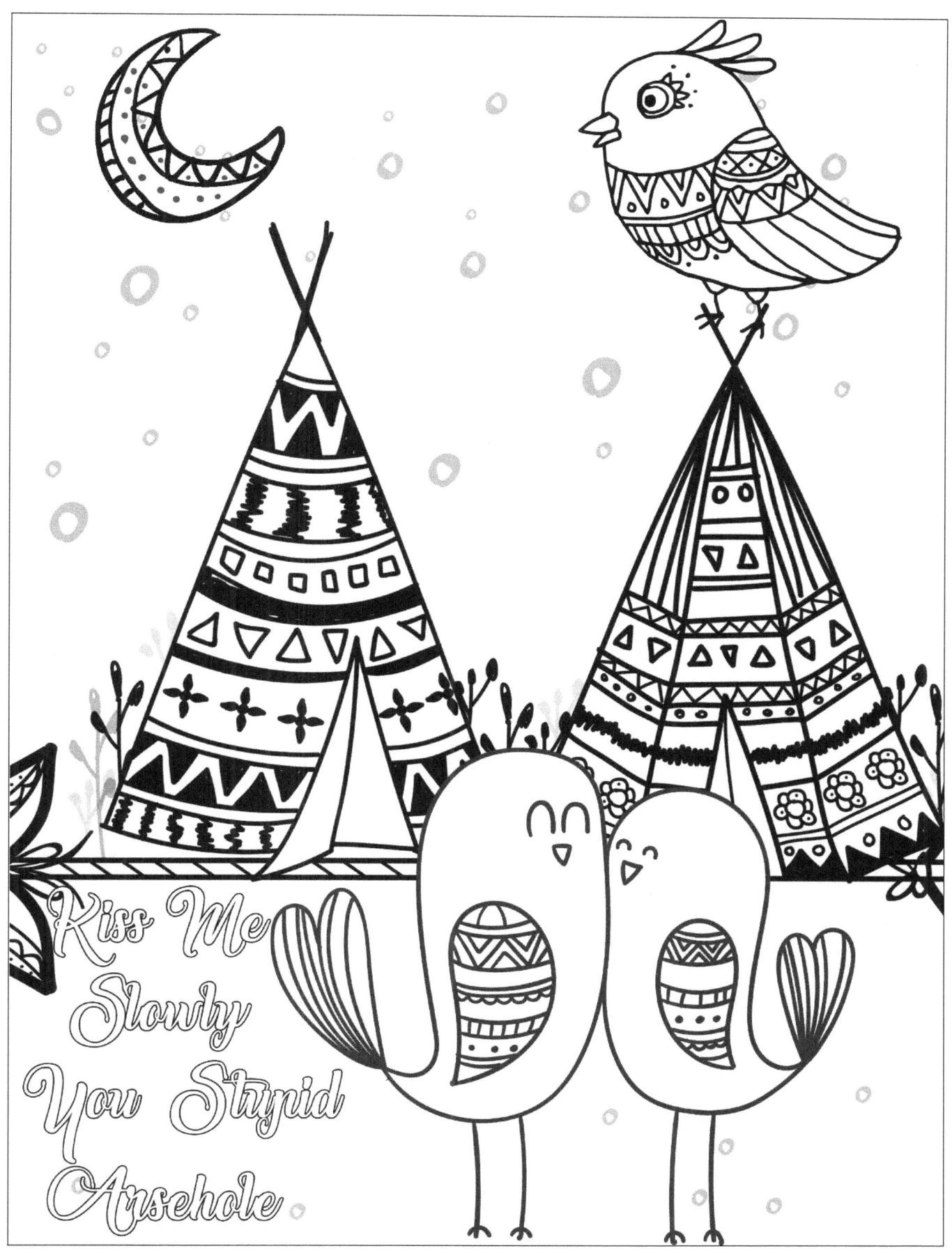

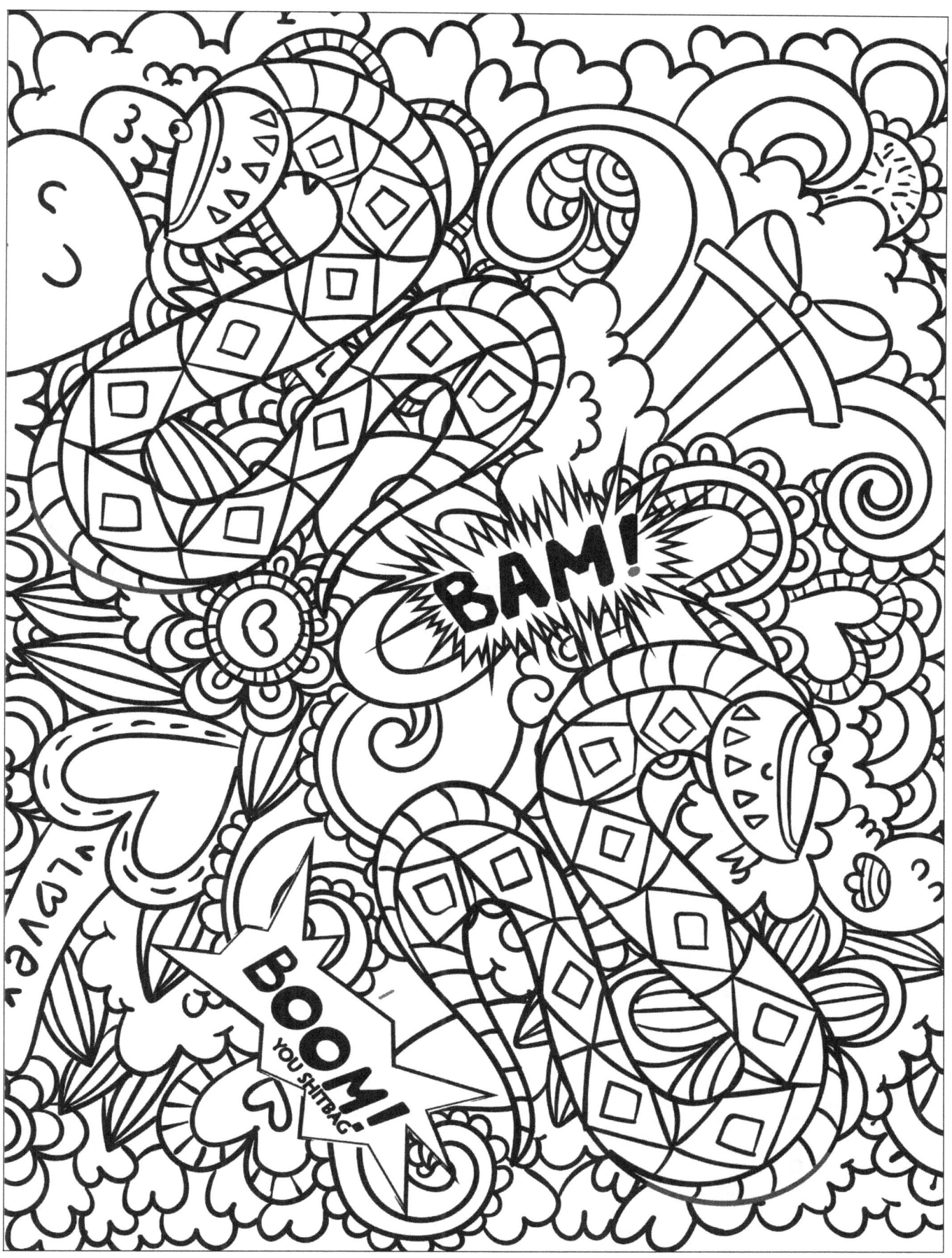

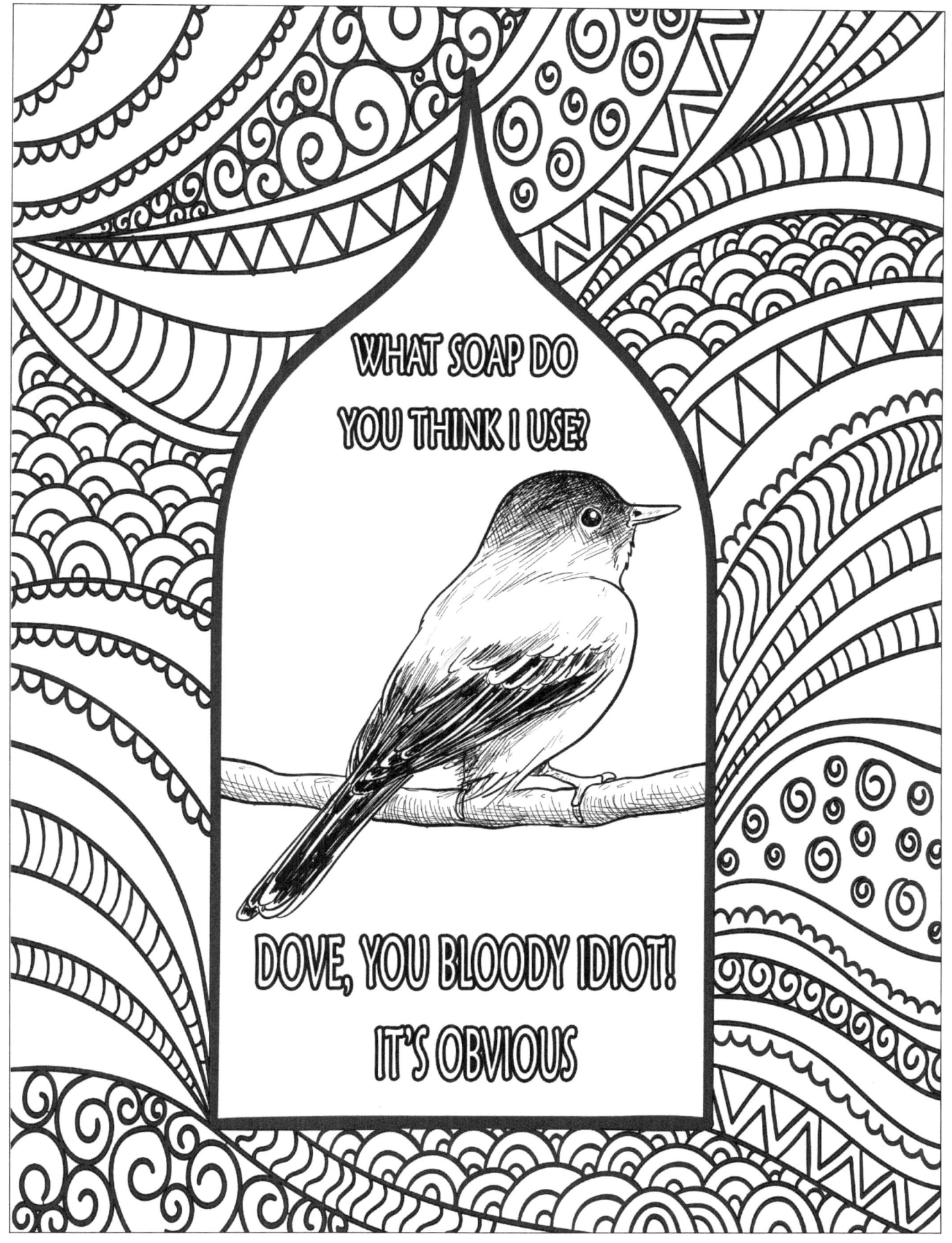

www.ingramcontent.com/pod-product-compliance
Lightning Source LLC
Chambersburg PA
CBHW081206180526
45170CB00006B/2240